Florence

Berlitz
Florence

Text: Patricia Schultz
Editor: Media Content Marketing, Inc.
Photography: Chris Coe except pages 13, 16, 27, 42, 48, 66, 68, 70, 76 by Jon Davison
Cover Photograph: Clive Sawyer/Pictures Colour Library
Photo Editor: Naomi Zinn
Layout: Media Content Marketing, Inc.
Cartography by Raffaelle Degennaro
Managing Editor: Tony Halliday

Elenenth Edition 2003

CONTACTING THE EDITORS
Every effort has been made to provide accurate information in this publication, but changes are inevitable. The publisher cannot be responsible for any resulting loss, inconvenience or injury. We would appreciate it if readers would call our attention to any errors or outdated information by contacting Berlitz Publishing, PO Box 7910, London SE1 1WE, England. Fax: (44) 20 7403 0290;
e-mail: berlitz@apaguide.demon.co.uk

010/311 RP

CONTENTS

● A (☞ in the text denotes a highly recommended sight

Florence

FLORENCE AND THE FLORENTINES

T he magnificent view from the hilltop church of San
Miniato has changed little since the 16th century. The
belvedere here looks out across the bridge-trellised Arno to
Florence's centro storico. It is a timeless sea of terracotta roof
tops interrupted only by the cupola of San Lorenzo, the medieval bell-tower of the Palazzo Vecchio and the focal point
that is Brunelleschi's massive Duomo. You are transported
back to the time of the Renaissance, when this Tuscan town
was one of the vital and most important cities in all of Europe.

The awesome contribution Florence made to Western civilization and culture is greatly out of proportion to its then
diminutive size. Few nations, let alone cities, can boast of having nurtured such a remarkable heritage of artistic, literary, sci-
entific and political talent in such a short period of time. Florence
was, as D.H. Lawrence put it, "man's perfect universe."
Centuries later, the names of Florence's greatest sons—Dante,
Boccaccio, Giotto, Donatello, Botticelli, Michelangelo,
Leonardo, Cellini, and Machiavelli—are still famous the world
over. It is an unparalleled record for any city—and one whose
uncontested period of greatness spanned less than 300 years.

Guidebooks often compare Renaissance Florence with fifth-
century B.C. Athens, but while the glory that was Greece is re-
called only by spectacular ruins, Renaissance Florence remains
very much in tact and in evidence at every turn. Its historic
palaces, great churches, exquisite sculptures, and countless
masterworks of art are not crumbling relics, but still a vivid and
functional part of everyday life—worked in, lived in, prayed
in, prized by present-day Florentines, and accessible to all.
Florence is an open-air museum, as loved by its proud residents
as it is revered by its foreign visitors.

Choosing souvenir postcards at the Piazza Duomo, in the shadow of the cathedral.

The elegant Palazzo Vecchio, where the first civic authority sat in the Middle Ages, still houses the offices of the city council. Congregations kneel for mass in churches commissioned by medieval guilds. The elegant jewelry stores lining the Ponte Vecchio are occupied by the descendants of goldsmiths who set up workshops here in the 14th century. Most of the city's narrow, cobbled side streets are the width necessary to permit the passage of horse-drawn carts of centuries ago. Not surprisingly, ever since the late 18th century, when Florence and its treasures became an unmissable stop on the "Grand Tour" undertaken by the British gentry, the city has proved irresistible to tourists. Today, the medieval alleys are lined with ice-cream bars and pizza shops, while postcard vendors and souvenir stalls crowd the piazzas, and milling throngs of visitors from around the world cram the streets and museums. But the bronze worker, lute maker, or leather artisan, although a dying breed, can still be found here in their workshops, recreating timeless crafts and arts whose roots reach back beyond the Medicis.

Florence's detractors describe the city as overcrowded and overpriced, and there is some modicum of truth in such criticisms. But the crowds, and to a certain extent the high prices, can be avoided by visiting in low season. And you'll never escape the overwhelming impact of so much superlative art and architecture, even if you have only a few days to see it. Be selective, pick out a few highlights, and absorb them at your leisure (see pages 78–80). If you try to cover everything, you'll end up exhausted, and remembering little.

The medieval Florentines were described as pragmatic, hard-working, inventive, and sharp-witted. These qualities are still evident in today's inhabitants, along with an inborn sense of dignity, elegance, a biting wit, and a savage pride in their city and its patrimony. The Florentines' renowned resilience has been illustrated repeatedly throughout history, but never more clearly than during the disastrous flood of November 1966 (the worst of many floods suffered by the city). Swollen by heavy rains, the Arno burst its banks one night, carrying away everything in its wake. In certain parts of the city the water reached depths of 7 m (23 ft)—small plaques around town indicate the height of the waters. Thick mud, mixed with damaging oil from ruptured tanks, swirled into basements and first-floor rooms of stores, museums, and homes. Hundreds of paintings, frescoes, and sculptures, and more than a million priceless antique books suffered incalculable damage, many beyond repair.

Before the flood waters had receded, the people of Florence rose to the challenge and joined in the herculean task of rescuing what they could. In the aftermath, they helped with the work of clearing debris and repairing the urban fabric; the impossible job of restoring damaged paintings and sculptures was in the hands of an international team of the art world's finest experts (some of them still working until this day). Most works are once again on display in the city museums and galleries.

The people's resolve was tested once again in May 1993, when a terrorist car bomb (its motive still enveloped in controversy, although conjecture abounds) tore apart the west wing of the Uffizi Gallery. Because it happened after-hours when the museum was closed, casualties were limited: the custodian and her family of four were killed. Thanks to protective plexiglass shields, irreparable damage was limited. Two hundred works were damaged, 37 of them seriously, and remarkably only two beyond repair. Almost before the dust had settled, repairs were underway. The Uffizi's 150-member staff worked around the clock without extra pay, putting the building back in order as soon as possible. As a result, a portion of the gallery was reopened to the public less than two months later. A further multi-million dollar restoration was completed in 1998, bringing the Uffizi and the heritage of the Medici into the new millennium.

It is this sense of being custodians of the legacy of the Renaissance, and heirs to an unmatched tradition of excellence, that gives the Florentines an almost Medici-like pride in their city. This feeling of continuity with the past is what makes Florence such a uniquely evocative place for visitors. Its unparalleled masterworks are not viewed simply as isolated museum pieces, but in the context of the city that produced them. They are a living record of an extraordinary period of creativity and innovation never seen or reproduced anywhere else in the world, at any time before or since. For this alone, Florence deserves all the superlatives that are shamelessly showered upon it. What's more, if the heat, crowds, and queues become too much you can always escape to a hilltop across the river, and savour the same view that Michelangelo must have savoured four and a half centuries ago.

A BRIEF HISTORY

No one quite knows how the Roman town of Florentia came by its name. According to some, it was named after Florinus, a Roman general, who in 63 B.C. encamped on the city's future site to besiege the nearby hill town of Fiesole ruled by the Etruscans, Italy's pre-Roman lords. Others maintain that the name refers to the abundance of flowers in the region, or perhaps even to the "flourishing" of the successful riverside town.

Whatever the origin of its name, Roman Florence developed into a thriving military and commercial settlement around 59 B.C. If you take a walk along the aptly named Via Romana on the south bank of the Arno and cross the Ponte Vecchio, toward the city center, you'll be following in the steps of the Roman legions, travelers, and merchants of two thousand years ago. And even though you'll find no visible Roman remains in Florence (although neighboring Fiesole boasts a number of Etruscan and Roman ruins dating to the first century B.C.), all the trappings of civilized Roman life were once located here, including a forum, baths, temples, and a theater.

However, a few centuries later, barbarian invasions and the fall of the Roman empire (A.D. 476) plunged Europe into a dark and turbulent period of history. A ray of light shone briefly during the sway of the Frankish king, Charlemagne and his vast European empire of the eighth and ninth centuries. By the tenth century, even greater chaos had set in.

Somehow the Carolingian province of Tuscany survived. In the late 11th century, Florence made rapid commercial and political progress under a remarkable ruler, Matilda, the Margrave of Tuscany. The great guilds (*arti maggiori*) — influential bodies set up to protect the interests of the apothecaries and the wool, silk, and spice merchants (among others) that were precursors of today's unions — came into being. By 1138, just 23 years after Matilda's death, Florence had developed into a self-governing republic and a power to be reckoned with.

At that time, Florence presented an appearance very different from that of today's city. The wealthy merchant families fortified their homes with square stone towers, often more than 70 m (230 ft) high, to serve as impregnable refuges during the recurring feuds that split the community. By the end of the 12th century, the city's skyline bristled with over 150 towers. Only a few have survived, but an idea of the town's early appearance can be grasped in the Tuscan hill town of San Gimignano, dubbed the "Medieval Manhattan" for its unique skyline (see page 76).

Guelphs and Ghibellines

Sooner or later the interests of an aristocratic elite and a rising merchant class were bound to clash, and when they did, Florence's development declined into a series of savage factional struggles. The nobility opposed the broader-based forms of government that the merchants sought to promote, and the situation was aggravated by fierce inter-family feuds and continual raids on Florentine trade by "robber barons."

To make matters worse, powerful foreign interests became involved. The Guelph and Ghibelline parties, which first developed in the 13th century, had their origins in other Italian cities, where the ambitions of the Papacy and the Holy Roman Empire (founded in A.D. 962) were diverging dangerously — the Guelphs supported the Pope (then a strong political figurehead), while the Ghibellines took the side of the Emperor. Further complicating matters was the French monarchy, which took an especially keen interest in Florentine developments, and was always ready to interfere in (and profit from) the internecine strife.

Other Tuscan cities soon followed suit with their own Guelph-Ghibelline factions and Tuscany remained in a state of turmoil for more than two centuries. Pisa, Lucca, Pistoia, Siena, Arezzo, and Florence became in turn enemies or allies, depending on which party held power in which town.

Yet in spite of these setbacks, Florentine commerce and banking continued to develop, and its woolen-cloth trade prospered. The first gold *fiorino* was minted in the mid-13th century. With the city's patron St. Giovanni on one side and the symbolic Florentine lily on the other, it was rapidly adopted throughout Europe as the standard unit of currency. The city's social evolution during this time was also remarkable: Organized "factories" or workshops, were opened; hospitals, schools, and charitable societies were founded; the university (one of Europe's oldest) turned out lawyers, teachers, and doctors; streets were paved, and laws were passed regulating noise and nuisance; and the Brotherhood of the Misericordia, a forerunner of the Red Cross (see page 26), was established. Although life was hard and Florence was never a democracy in the modern sense of the word, the city gave its citizens a unique sense of "belonging" that overcame class or party differences.

A heavenly tribute adorns the ceiling of the Medici Chapel of the Princes.

In spite of their internal divisions, the Guelphs gradually edged the Ghibellines out of power. By the late 13th century, the bankers, merchants, and city guilds had a firm grasp on the helm of the Florentine republic, and felt secure enough to turn their attention to the building of a fitting seat of government. Already involved with the construction of a sumptuous cathedral, a mighty People's Palace — the Palazzo del Popolo — was begun in 1298. This was later called the Palazzo della Signoria and is now known as the Palazzo Vecchio. Located in the Piazza della Signoria, it still serves as the city hall (after having followed a brief stint as a Medici residence during the Renaissance); it is one of the most handsome structures from this period still in existence.

Dawn of a Golden Age

Florentine bankers now held the purse-strings of Europe, with agents in every major city. One group, headed by the Bardi and Peruzzi families, lent Edward III of England 1,365,000 gold florins to finance his campaigns against the French. Then in 1343 the double-dealing Edward suddenly declared himself bankrupt, and toppled the entire banking system.

As always, the resilient Florentines recovered, and the merchant interests set out with ruthless zeal to regain their lost prestige. Despite ceaseless social unrest, violent working-class riots, disastrous floods, and the Black Death of 1347–1348, which claimed half the city's population (and one third of Italy's), by the early 1400s Florence found itself stronger and richer than ever. The foundation had been laid for its brightest moment to come.

The city's cultural life was flourishing, moving toward the early years of what was to become known as the Renaissance.

Interest in long-neglected Greek and Latin literature was being revived. While Florentine historians started recording their city's progress for posterity, merchant guilds and the nouveau riche found time between business deals and party vendettas to indulge in artistic patronage.

Despite factional divisions, the Florentines were able to plan ambitious public works and awe-inspiring private palazzos: The Duomo, Giotto's Campanile, the great monastic churches of Santa Croce and Santa Maria Novella, the Bargello, and the Palazzo Vecchio were all begun or completed during the tumultuous 14th century.

A putto with dolphin frolic in a fountain in the courtyard of the Palazzo Vecchio.

The power of the important business families, the *signori*, was slowly proving to be greater than that of the guilds. The ambitious Medici family of wealthy wool merchants and bankers (and not doctors, as their family name implies) came to dominate every facet of Florentine life for 60 golden years (1434–1494) and, to a diminishing degree, decades thereafter. Shrewd politicians and enthusiastic and discerning patrons of the arts, they led the city and its people to unparalleled heights of civilization, at a time when most of Europe was struggling to free itself from the coarse, tangled mesh of medieval feudalism.

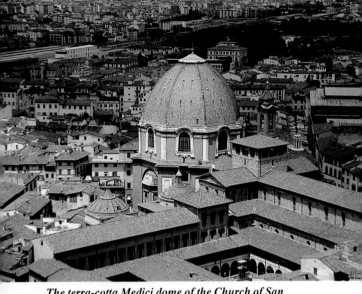

The terra-cotta Medici dome of the Church of San Lorenzo is a highlight of the centro storico's skyline.

The Renaissance

The term "Renaissance" *(Rinascimento)* was coined by 16th-century Florentine artist and historian Giorgio Vasari (1511–1574), whose book *Lives of the Most Excellent Painters, Sculptors and Architects* tells almost everything we know about the great Italian artists from the 13th century up to his own time (some historians believe the expression came into use much later). "Renaissance" means "rebirth," which is exactly how Vasari saw the events of the 15th century — the world appeared to be waking from a long sleep and taking up life where antiquity had left off. The Church had dominated the cultural life of Europe throughout the Middle Ages.

Literature, architecture, painting, sculpture, and music were all aimed at the glorification of God, rather than the celebration of earthly life and beauty. The Greek and Roman concept of "art for art's sake" had been forgotten until it was revived in 15th-century Florence. As you visit the Uffizi Gallery, compare Cimabue's *Virgin Enthroned* (c. 1290) with Botticelli's *Primavera* (1477–1478), which illustrate the difference between the art of the Middle Ages and the Renaissance.

The idea had taken hold that life must be lived to its fullest and that the pursuit of earthly knowledge, beauty, and pleasure were what counted most in the brief time allotted to man. The arts and sciences of the Renaissance were directed toward those ends.

The Medici Influence

Although few of the early Medici ever held office in the city government, three of them were in fact the true rulers of Florence. They were: Cosimo, *Il Vecchio* ("the Elder," 1389–1464), a munificent patron of the arts and letters and founder of the Medici dynasty, who earned himself the title *pater patriae* ("father of his country"); his son, Piero, *Il Gottoso* ("the Gouty," 1416–1469); and his grandson Lorenzo, *Il Magnifico* ("the Magnificent," 1449–1492). Ably pulling strings via supporters elected to the republican government (the *Signoria*), all three were expert politicians who knew how to win the hearts and minds of the Florentine masses.

Poet, naturalist, art collector, dabbler in philosophy, and would-be architect (a fine example of what is still referred to as a "Renaissance man"), Lorenzo was perhaps the most outstanding member of the Medici dynasty. His diplomatic skill kept Italy temporarily free of wars and invasions and his love of the arts effected cultural life as we know it today.

On Lorenzo's death in 1492, his son Piero took his place. Loutish and devoid of taste, Piero was deemed unworthy of the Medici name; he lasted only two years. When Charles VIII of France invaded Italy, Piero first opposed him but suddenly changed sides as it became clear that the French were winning. He had to accept humiliating terms of settlement. The Florentine people were so enraged that they drove him from the city and set up a republic. It was at this time that Niccolo Machiavelli held office in Florence, gaining first-hand experience in the arts of intrigue and diplomacy.

The spiritual force behind the new republic was a fanatical Dominican friar, Girolamo Savonarola (1452–1498). Prior of the Monastery of San Marco, he preached regularly in the Duomo during Lorenzo's last years. Audiences of thousands heard him inveigh against the excesses of the Medici courts, prophesying apocalyptic punishments for the city if its people did not embrace a more godly way of life. In 1494, he decreed the destruction of the "vanities"

Florentine Explorers

Amerigo Vespucci (1454–1512) went down in history as the man who gave his name to America. Banker, businessman, and navigator, he crossed the Atlantic in the wake of Christopher Columbus (from Genoa), and explored the coast of South America, discovering the estuaries of the Orinoco and Rio de la Plata. His main achievement was to ascertain that Columbus had, in fact, discovered a "New World," and not Asia, as Columbus himself had maintained.

More than 20 years later, another Florentine navigator, Giovanni da Verrazzano (1485–1528), searching for the legendary Northwest Passage, sailed through the narrows that now bear his name, and discovered New York Harbor.

of art, and Florentines flocked to the Piazza della Signoria with armfuls of illuminated books, hand-loomed textiles, and precious paintings, which they hurled upon a huge bonfire in the middle of the square. Even Botticelli joined in, flinging some of his own paintings into the flames. But Savonarola had powerful enemies (Pope Borgia, for one) who soon brought about his downfall. He was arrested, sentenced to death for heresy, and hanged and burned where his "bonfire of the vanities" had taken place four years earlier; a bronze plaque still marks the spot in Piazza della Signoria.

In 1512, Piero's brothers, Giovanni and Giuliano, returned to Florence, putting an end to the republic. Expelled in 1527, the persistent Medici were back three years later, after an eight-month siege, with the help of the Holy Roman Emperor Charles V. During the subsequent rule of grand-duke Cosimo I de' Medici (1537–1574), an attempt was made to revive the spirit of the Medici's earlier golden age. Some of Florence's most prominent monuments date from this period, including the Santa Trinita Bridge, Boboli Gardens (Cosimo's backyard gardens when residing in the Palazzo Pitti), the Neptune Fountain in the Piazza della Signoria, and Cellini's magnificent bronze Perseus, whose copy stands in the Loggia dei Lanzi in Piazza della Signoria.

A New Role

Under the rule of the grand dukes of Tuscany (Medici until 1743, then Hapsburgs up to 1859), Florence sank into a torpor which lasted for more than three centuries. Anna Maria Ludovica, last of the Medici line who died in 1749, made a grand final gesture worthy of her Renaissance forebears. Farsightedly, she bequeathed the entire Medici art collection (the

Views from the Piazzale Michelangelo show a cross-section of Florentine history.

basis of the staggering collection of the Uffizi Gallery, formerly the offices of the Medici) to the city "to attract foreigners," on condition that none of it ever be sold or removed from Florence. Her wish was granted, for the foreigners came, at first a small but steady trickle of privileged young gentlemen doing the Grand Tour of Europe, the traditional finishing touch to a gentleman's cultural education.

In the 19th century, a new breed of traveler appeared — the "Italianate Englishman," led by the poets Byron and Shelley, and followed by the Brownings, John Ruskin, and the Pre-Raphaelites. Rapturous Britons, smitten by the romantic image of Italy, toured or settled in droves, bringing in their wake French, German, and Russian tourists, all referred to as "the English" by the Florentines. Queen Victoria herself visited the city. Florence Nightingale was named for the city of her birth (there is a statue of her in the Santa Croce cloister); she would go on to claim her fame in the Crimean War.

After the dramatic events of the Risorgimento, when the occupying Austrians were expelled, Florence had a brief moment of glory as the capital of the newly unified kingdom of Italy

(1865–1871). With the transfer of the capital to Rome, the story of Florence merges into Italian history.

The 20th Century and Beyond

Despite the excitement at the time of unification, democracy failed to become firmly established in Italy. Crisis followed crisis, and the people lost confidence in the nascent government. During World War I, Italy fought against Germany and Austria, but afterwards the country felt it had been insufficiently rewarded for its sacrifices. As parliamentary democracy disintegrated, Benito Mussolini seized power in 1922 and declared himself prime minister of Italy.

With the Rome-Berlin Axis of 1937, Mussolini linked the fate of Italy to that of Hitler's Germany, dragging his country into defeat in World War II. The Fascist government fell in 1943, and some of the most heroic battles of the Italian resistance were fought in and around Florence. The retreating Germans blew up all the bridges over the Arno except for the Ponte Vecchio, spared, it is believed, because of its famous past (this didn't stop the Germans from destroying the bridge-heads on either side, however). The city's art treasures and landmark architecture survived unscathed. Mussolini and his mistress were executed in Milan in 1945.

Present-day Florence is an important business center and university city (the large number of foreign students is explained by 20-odd year-abroad programs of various foreign universities), as well as a major tourist mecca. Its suburbs boast a versatile array of automobile, textile, and small manufacturing industries.

Conscious of their position as the inheritors of a great creative and artistic tradition, the heirs of the Medici are striving to keep their city alive and vibrant, at the forefront of the world of art, literature, and fashion.

WHERE TO GO

I t's all too easy to be intimidated by the sheer quantity of art and architecture in Florence—there are nearly 70 museums and art galleries, and 24 historic churches, as well as shops, restaurants, piazzas, and countless side-streets to explore. (See page 78 for our list of the major churches, palaces, museums, and galleries.)

For those with more time to spare, we've divided the city into four walking tours, each of which can be covered in a day (take into consideration high-season lines at some museums).

THE DUOMO TO THE PONTE VECCHIO

The historic heart of Florence, the **centro storico,** is a grid of narrow streets between the Duomo (cathedral) and the River Arno. Many of the city's famous sights lie in this area, within easy walking distance from each other.

Piazza del Duomo/Piazza San Giovanni

A short stroll from Santa Maria Novella railway station will bring you to Piazza Duomo, where you get your first, very impressive sight of Florentine religious architecture: The huge multi-colored façade of the **Duomo** rises majestically alongside the pointed roof of the Baptistery (see page 25).

Officially known as *Santa Maria dei Fiori* (Saint Mary of the Flowers), the Duomo was designed by the great architect Arnolfo di Cambio (1245–1302) who was also responsible for the Palazzo Vecchio, and was intended to surpass all the great buildings of antiquity in size and splendor.

Work began around 1296 on the site of the far smaller fifth-century cathedral of Santa Reparata, but was not completed until the second half of the 15th century; its elaborate, Neo-Gothic façade was added as late as the 19th century. Like most

Tuscan churches of the time, the Duomo presents a unique local version of Gothic-style architecture, not easily compared to northern European ecclesiastical buildings of the same period.

The mighty **cupola** was the contribution of Filippo Brunelleschi (1377–1446; see page 53), the first true "Renaissance" architect. He had marveled at the dome on Rome's Pantheon, rebuilt for Emperor Hadrian about A.D. 125.

When the ambitious Florentines decided that their showpiece cathedral must have a great dome, they held

A good place for a stroll: the Piazza di San Giovanni and adjoining Piazza Duomo.

a public competition in 1418. Brunelleschi submitted the winning design (encouraged by the organizers to make it *il più bello che si può*—as beautiful as possible) and, just as important, a workable building scheme. (The original wooden model of the dome is in the Museo dell'Opera del Duomo; see page 26.) In Florence, where beauty and art were never the preserve of the rich alone, these competitions used to cause immense, popular excitement. Citizens—rich and poor, high and low—often sat together on the panel of judges.

Brunelleschi's truly magnificent dome, the first giant cupola since antiquity, was finally completed in 1436. It was visible for miles, dwarfing the red-tiled rooftops around it, and confirming the feeling of the day that nothing was beyond the science and ingenuity of Man. In late 1996, a 15-year restoration of the 16th century fresoces covering the inside of the cupola was completed. Begun by Giorgio Vasari and finished by his less-brilliant student Federico Zuccari, the original fresco is the world's largest depiction of the Last Supper. You can climb up (there is no elevator) the spiraling 463 steps to the top of the lantern and enjoy breath-taking panoramic views over the city.

Most of the Duomo's original statuary (from both the facade and interior) was long ago removed to the Museo dell' Opera del Duomo for safe keeping. There are neverthe-less some important works of art to be seen within the cathe-dral. Make sure you see Lorenzo Ghiberti's bronze shrine, below the high altar, which was made to house the remains of St. Zenobius (one of Florence's first bishops). The three stained-glass rose windows on the entrance wall of the Duomo were also designed by the versatile Ghiberti.

Left of the entrance are some rather unusual *trompe l'oeil* frescoes of two 15th-century *condottieri*, or mercenary cap-tains, who fought for Florence. The right-hand one, painted by that great master of perspective, Paolo Uccello, com-memorates an Englishman, John Hawkwood, the only for-eigner ever buried in the Duomo. Uccello is also responsible for the 1443 **ora italica** clock next to Ghiberti's windows.

If you're lucky enough to be at the Duomo on Easter Sunday, you can witness the famous, centuries-old ceremony of *Scoppio del Carro* (Explosion of the Cart, see page 90).

The Duomo's free-standing **Campanile** (bell-tower) is one of Florence's most graceful landmarks. It was begun in 1334 by the multi-talented genius Giotto, and completed in 1359 by his successors Andrea Pisano and Andrea Talenti. Faced in green, white, and pink marble to match the Duomo, the low-est story bears Giotto-designed reliefs illustrating the

Creation of Man, and the *Arti* (guilds) and Industries of Florence by Pisano and Luca Della Robbia. The niches in the second story contain statues of the Prophets and Sibyls, some of them by Donatello. The originals of almost all of these statues are to be found in the Museo dell'Opera del Duomo (see page 26). It's worth making the 414-step climb to the top for a bird's-eye view of the cathedral and a city that was never permitted to build higher than the cathedral's dome.

Opposite the Duomo lies **Il Battistero** (The Baptistery). Acclaimed as the oldest building in Florence, this precious gem of octagonal Romanesque architecture, built in the early 12th century on what is believed to be the site of a Roman temple, served for a time as Florence's cathedral. With the exception of its doors, the exterior appearance remains as it was in the time of Dante. Brilliant Byzantine 13th-century mosaics inside the cupola include scenes from the *Creation*, *Life of St. John,* and an 8-m (26-ft) Christ in the *Last Judgement.*

The Baptistery's principal claim to fame is its three sets of gilded bronze doors. Those on the south side are the oldest: Dating from the 14th century, they are the work of Andrea Pisano. Those on the north (facing Via Cavour) and east (facing the Duomo's main entrance, and therefore the most important) were

The east door of Il Battistero, otherwise known as "The Gates of Paradise."

made by Lorenzo Ghiberti in the first half of the 15th century while he was still a young man.

A competition to design the east doors was held in 1401, financed by one of the richest merchant guilds (then a common practice). Brunelleschi was among those who submitted an entry, but Ghiberti's submission (what you now see as the north doors) was unanimously declared the winner. The two sculptors' original entries are exhibited in the Bargello (see page 29), so you can judge for yourself.

The east doors, facing the Duomo, were later described by an admiring Michelangelo as being fit to be the **"Gates of Paradise."** The name has stuck ever since. (These doors are actually copies—the original panels have been restored and are now on display in the Museo dell'Opera del Duomo.)

On the corner of Via dei Calzaiuoli, south of the Baptistery, is the graceful 14th-century **Loggia del Bigallo,** once part of the headquarters of a society for the care of orphans. Across the street (to the east of Via Calzaiuoli) lies the headquarters of one of Florence's oldest and most respected social institutions, the Brotherhood of the Misericordia. Founded by St. Peter Martyr in 1244, it was especially needed during frequent bouts of pestilence and plagues. Today's unpaid volunteers, easily recognized in their black hooded capes, provide free assistance to the poor and needy, and also run Florence's emergency ambulance service. Respectful visits are permitted.

At the east end of the Piazza Duomo, the **Museo dell'Opera del Duomo** is the Duomo's own museum, where many of its most precious treasures and original sculptures have been taken for safekeeping. A renovation, completed in 1998, has just doubled its size. Highlights include a sumptuous 14th-/15th-century silver-faced altar from the Baptistery; rich gold and silver reliquaries (one of which houses the index finger of St. John, Florence's patron saint); Brunelleschi's original wooden model of the Duomo's cupola; Donatello's harrowing wooden effigy of Mary Magdalen and the *Zuccone* that once graced the Campanile; and two beautiful sculptured choir lofts (*cantorie*), one by Donatello and the other by Luca della Robbia. Here, too, is housed Michelangelo's unfinished *Pietà*; it is said that he intended it for his own tomb.

Via dell' Oriuolo, off the southeast corner of Piazza del Duomo, leads to the **Museo "Firenze com'era"** ("Florence as it was"), where you will find a great number of paintings, prints, and photographs illustrating the city's history.

Back in Piazza Duomo, take the narrow Via del Proconsolo southward to visit the forbidding, fortress-like Palazzo del

This view from the Duomo's cupola features the Palazzo del Bargello, home of Florentine justice in the Middle Ages.

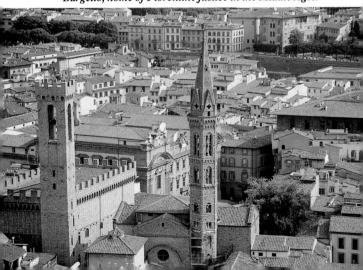

Bargello, home of the **Museo Nazionale del Bargello.** Florence's original town hall and one of its earliest public buildings (begun c. 1250), the Bargello served as the seat of the magistrates (*podestà*) responsible for law and order, and later housed the office of the Captain of Justice (*bargello*), the 16th century equivalent of today's police commissioner.

Criminals were imprisoned, tortured, and executed here. Cages were often hung outside with tortured prisoners as a warning to would-be wrongdoers and as targets for a stone-and-fruit-throwing public. Today, the Bargello is to sculpture what the Uffizi is to painting, for it houses many Renaissance masterpieces. The first room beyond the entrance is the **Sala Michelangelo** (Hall of Michelangelo)—note the marks on the wall recording the water level of the 1966 flood at 3 m (9 ft).

Michelangelo was only 21 when he finished his early masterpiece, *The Drunken Bacchus.* He sculpted the marble *Pitti Tondo* of the Virgin and Child eight years later, in 1504, while working on his famous *David* (now in the Accademia). You will

also find Michelangelo's "other David," a.k.a. *Apollo*, sculpted 30 years after the original. For a portrait of the artist, see Daniele da Volterra's bronze bust of Michelangelo at his dourest.

A door leads into the attractive courtyard, softened by the brownish hues of its *pietra forte*, and covered

Ponder the work of the Old Masters, such as Verrochio, at the Bargello museum.

with a *mélange* of stone plaques bearing the arms of successive *podestà*. A 14th-century stone staircase leads to an arcaded loggia on the first floor, where you'll see Giambologna's series of remarkably lifelike bronze birds surrounding a marble figure representing Architecture.

The first-floor exhibits include Italian and Tuscan ceramics, old Murano glass, French Limoges enamels, and astonishing, delicate engraved seashells. The 14th-century chapel contains frescoes painted by a pupil of Giotto (the sharp-featured man behind the kneeling figure on the right is said to be Dante).

If you are pressed for time, head straight for the **Sala di Consiglio Generale (Great Hall),** which contains works that capture the spirit of early-Renaissance Florence. Donatello's movingly human *St. George* (1416) dominates the back wall of this high-vaulted room. Commissioned by the armorers' guild as their contribution to the exterior decorations of Orsanmichele (see page 40), its depth and sense of movement are generally believed to represent the first great sculptural achievement of the Renaissance.

Donatello's most important work—his bronze *David* (1440–1450)—is credited as the first free-standing nude statue of the Renaissance. In contrast to the "modern" feeling of *St. George,* the *David* has an antique and ambiguous sensuality about it, while the delightful bronze *Amore* (cupid) is positively Roman in style. More personal and dramatic are the two marble versions of *St. John the Baptist*.

Be sure to take a look at Ghiberti's and Brunelleschi's original bronze panels (*The Sacrifice of Abraham*) for the Baptistery design competition of 1401 (see page 26); they're on the right wall towards the back of the rooom.

The Sala di Verrocchio on the second floor has Verrocchio's bronze *David* (c. 1471), which is said to have been modeled on the sculptor's 19-year-old pupil, Leonardo da Vinci.

Across the street from the Bargello is the church known as the **Badia Fiorentina,** with its graceful bell-tower, part Romanesque, part Gothic. Go inside for a moment to admire Filipino Lippi's delightful *Madonna Appearing to St. Bernard*, on the left of the church as you enter.

Piazza della Signoria

Continue south from the Bargello through the small Piazza San Firenze and turn right into Via dei Gondi, which leads to the wide expanse of the **Piazza della Signoria**.

A copy of Michelangelo's "David" (left) at the entrance of the Palazzo Vecchio.

If the Piazza del Duomo is the religious heart of Florence, this piazza is its political and social counterpart. The city rulers have gathered here since the 13th century, and the present-day offices of the city council are still housed in the austere Palazzo Vecchio. In summer the square is crowded with tourists, visiting the Palazzo and the neighboring Uffizi, admiring the wealth of statues, enjoying a drink in the open-air cafés, and having their pictures taken amid the Florentine pigeons.

Dominating the square is the fortress-like **Palazzo Vecchio**, which is also known as the Palazzo della Signoria, after the highest tier of the city's 15th-century Republican government, known as the *Signoria*, which convened here. Designed by Arnolfo di Cambio, the architect who designed the Duomo, and intended to house the city's government, it served briefly as a royal Medici residence. It acquired the name Palazzo Vecchio (Old Palace) after 1549, when the Medici moved their headquarters across the river to the Palazzo Pitti (see page 62).

The palazzo's off-center 94-m (308-ft) tower, added in 1310, helps to soften the squareness of the late-Gothic palazzo, and complements its own off-center position on the piazza. The ornate courtyard of the palazzo comes as a surprise after the medieval austerity of the exterior. Verrocchio's bronze fountain depicting a *putto* (cherub) with a dolphin was brought from Lorenzo de' Medici's villa at Careggi. What you see here is a copy; the original is displayed upstairs.

The palazzo's highlights include the massive **Salone dei Cinquecento,** on the first floor. Built to house the parliament

Begun in 1299, the fortress-like Palazzo Vecchio towers above the Piazza della Signoria

of the short-lived Florentine republic declared in 1494 (see page 18), it was turned into a grand throne room by Cosimo I, and decorated with giant Vasari frescoes of Florentine victories and Michelangelo's statue *The Genius of Victory,* representing Cosimo's triumph over enemy Siena in 1554–1555. Three centuries later, the first parliament of a united Italy met here. It is still used today for special government functions.

A small door to the right of the main entrance allows visitors to peek into the **Studiolo di Francesco I,** a little gem of a study designed by Vasari. It is covered from floor to barrel-vaulted ceiling with painted allegorical panels (representing Fire, Water, Earth, and Air), and two Bronzino portraits of Cosimo I and his consort gazing down haughtily.

Across the hall, another door leads into the **Quartiere di Leone X,** the apartments of Leo X (the first Medici pope). The rooms are sumptuously decorated with frescoes celebrating the heroic achievements of the Medici family. Stairs lead up to the equally sumptuous **Quartiere degli Elementi,** with painted allegories on the theme of the elements. The Terraza di Saturno at the back provides a fine view across the river to San Miniato and the Forte di Belvedere.

A dizzying gallery above the Salone dei Cinquecento connects with the **Quartiere di Eleonora** (the apartments of Eleonora of Toledo, Cosimo I's Spanish wife), a riot of gilt, painted ceilings, and rich furnishings.

The splendid 15th-century **Sala dei Gigli** (Hall of the Lilies), all blue and gold, is lavishly decorated with Florentine heraldry, a gilt-paneled ceiling, bright Ghirlandaio frescoes, and superb doors inlaid with figures of Dante and Petrarch. Here stands Donatello's original bronze of *Judith and Holofernes* (a copy of it is in the piazza outside).

The adjoining **Cancelleria,** used as an office by Machiavelli, now houses a lifelike, colored bust and portrait of the author of

The Prince. Next door is the splendid **Guardaroba** or **Sala Mappamondo**, a cupboard-lined room whose wooden panels were painted with maps by two learned Dominican friars (1563–1587). The 57 maps illustrate the extent of the world known to Western civilization in the late 16th century.

To the right of the Palazzo Vecchio and on the south side of the Piazza della Signoria is the **Loggia della Signoria,** or **Loggia dei Lanzi** (also called Loggia di Orcagna after the architect), built in the late 14th century. Originally a covered vantage point for city officials at public ceremonies, it took its later name from Cosimo I's Swiss-German

"Rape of the Sabines" is one of many fine sculptures in the Loggia dei Lanzi.

mercenary bodyguards, known as *Landsknechts* (Italianized to *Lanzichenecchi*); they used it as a guard-room during his nine-year residence in the Palazzo Vecchio. Since the late 18th century the loggia has been used as an open-air museum of sculpture, but celebrated works of art have been displayed here since long before then. Cellini's fine bronze *Perseus* (which is now found in the Uffizi where it is undergoing restoration), was originally placed here, on Cosimo's order in 1554 (a copy replaced it in 1998). Giambologna's famous ***Rape of the Sabines*** was added in 1583, while his *Hercules and the Centaur* and the

Roman statues at the back, donated by the Medicis, were added toward the end of the 18th century.

In front of the palazzo a *marzocco*—a heraldic lion bearing the city's arms (the symbol of Florence)—has graced the piazza for almost as long as the palazzo itself (what you see today is a copy; the original is in the Bargello). Michelangelo's *David* was positioned here in 1504 as a Republican symbol but was moved to the Accademia (see page 46) in 1873 and replaced by a copy (the present version is a second copy, from the early 20th century; a bronze version can be found across the river in the Piazzale Michelangelo). The rather grotesque statue of *Hercules and Cacus* beside it is the work of a 16th-century sculptor, Bandinelli. It is given little attention, standing as it does in the shadow of David's magnificence.

☛ The Uffizi

Between the Palazzo Vecchio and the Arno, the imposing **Uffizi Gallery** stretches down either side of the narrow Piazzale degli Uffizi. Built by Vasari in the second half of the 16th century —it would be his greatest architectural work—the building was intended to house the headquarters of the various government offices (*uffizi* is old Italian for "offices"), the official mint, and workshops for Medici craftsmen. It is now the home of one of the world's most famous and important art galleries.

If you want to avoid the worst of the crowds, try to come in the late afternoon or early evening, after most of the tour groups have left. Also, tickets can now be purchased in advance by credit card (call Firenze Musei, Tel. (055) 29 48 83 Mon–Fri, before leaving home, or immediately upon your arrival in Florence), allowing you to avoid the achingly long lines which have become commonplace.

Exhibited in chronological order, the paintings comprise the cream of Italian and European art from the 13th to 18th

The exterior of the Uffizi gallery shows off an architectural style befitting one of the world's great museums.

centuries. Begun by Cosimo I and added to by his successors, the collection was bequeathed to the people of Florence in perpetuity in 1737 by Anna Maria Ludovica, the last of the Medici dynasty, on condition that it never leave the city. To avoid being overwhelmed by the sheer quantity of art, you should have no qualms about skipping some of the 33 or so rooms that lead off the two first-floor galleries. We have listed the highlights below. (Note that some positionings change due to continual restorations and rotating exhibits).

The first rooms contain those early Tuscan greats, Cimabue and Giotto. In their altarpieces depicting enthroned Madonnas (painted in the years 1280 and 1310, respectively), the mosaic-like stiffness of Cimabue's work contrasts vividly with Giotto's innovative depth and more expressive figures. The greatest painter of the 14th-century Sienese school was Simone Martini: This claim is evidenced by his graceful

Settignano's "St. John the Baptist" is one of the sublime figures at the Bargello.

Annunciation (1333), painted for Siena's cathedral. Of the later Italian Gothic masterpieces, Gentile da Fabriano's *Adoration of the Magi* (1423) is the most exquisite.

Among the best loved and most reproduced of Renaissance paintings are Botticelli's haunting *Primavera* (The Allegory of Springtime; 1477–1478) and his renowned *Birth of Venus* (commonly referred to as Venus on the Half-Shell, c. 1485). Botticelli's lifelike but theatrical *Adoration of the Magi* features portraits of the Medici family— Cosimo Il Vecchio, his son Piero Il Gottoso, and grandsons Lorenzo Il Magnifico and Giuliano (smugly standing on the extreme left, a few years before his murder). Botticelli himself, in a yellow cloak and golden curls, gazes out on the far right.

The following room is devoted to Leonardo da Vinci. The *Baptism of Christ* (c. 1474–1475) was mostly the work of his great teacher, Verrocchio. Although only the background and the angel on the left were the work of the 18-year-old Leonardo, when Verrocchio saw how exquisitely his pupil had rendered the angel, he swore never to touch a paintbrush again. The *Annunciation* (c. 1472–1477) is entirely Leonardo's work, as is the *Adoration of the Magi* (1481). The latter is not just unfinished, but barely begun, merely sketched out in preparatory *chiaroscuro*, or light and shade, but this is sufficient to show Leonardo's unique approach to the subject and his inherent talents.

Outstanding among the 15th-century Flemish paintings is Hugo Van der Goes' huge triptych *Adoration of the Shepherds* (1478), which was painted for the Medici's Flemish agent, Tommaso Portinari. The Portinari family is immortalized on its side-panels. In a sunnier, lighter vein is Ghirlandaio's *Adoration* (1487).

The octagonal room known as the Tribuna, commissioned by the Medici from Buontalenti, symbolizes the four elements. The sumptuous 17th-century inlaid stone table, specially made for the room, took 16 years to complete. Here also are Bronzino's portraits of Cosimo I's Spanish wife, *Eleonora of Toledo*, and their chubby, smiling baby son, Giovanni—one of the most famous child portraits ever painted.

The *Medici Venus*, a marble nude excavated at Hadrian's Tivoli villa, is thought to be a copy of a fourth-century-B.C. Greek original by Praxiteles. Said to represent Phryne, the notorious Athenian courtesan who became rich through her many lovers, it was supposedly Thomas Jefferson's favorite piece of sculpture, and he kept a copy of it in his study.

Among the German masterpieces in the Uffizi, look out for Dürer's *Portrait of His Father* (1490) and *Adoration of the Magi* (1504), and Cranach's lifelike little portraits of *Luther*, his renegade wife, and a solid *Adam and Eve* (1526).

Among the works of the 15th-century Venetian School are Bellini's strange, dream-like *Sacred Allegory*, painted about 1490 (curiously, its allegorical significance has never been satisfactorily explained).

The Uffizi contains just one work by the great Michelangelo—a round oil painting showing the Holy Family, known as the *Doni Tondo* (1503–1505). Firmly but humanly treated, it is the only known panel painting by the artist better known for frescoes and sculpture.

Equally notable are Raphael's maternal *Madonna del Cardellino* (Madonna of the Goldfinch; c. 1505) and a wistful self-portrait painted in Florence when he was only 23. The works by Titian includes *Flora* (c. 1515) and his celebrated, voluptuous nude, the *Venus of Urbino* (1538). (More works by Raphael and Titian are in the Palazzo Pitti.)

The final few rooms contain Caravaggio's splendidly decadent *Young Bacchus* (1589); and Rembrandt's famous *Portrait of an Old Rabbi*, as well as two self-portraits.

At the far end of the West Corridor is a newly renovated terrace cafe, which sits above the Loggia dei Lanzi overlooking the Piazza della Signoria.

☛ Ponte Vecchio

From the Uffizi exit, walk down to the river and turn right along the embankment. Above the pavement runs the Corridoio Vasariano, a graceful covered walkway built by Vasari in 1565 to link the Uffizi and the Palazzo Vecchio with the Medici's new headquarters in the Palazzo Pitti, so that Grand Duke Cosimo de' Medici could commute between the two without ever braving the elements. You can see the Corridoio continuing across the Ponte Vecchio above the shops. Its collection of portraits can be viewed during limited visiting hours and only upon advance request: Inquire at the Uffizi box office window.

The oldest bridge in Florence, the **Ponte Vecchio** was the only one spared destruction during World War II (though both sides of its banks were bombed; notice how the buildings are of a 1950s vintage). The present bridge, lined with elitist jewelers' and goldsmiths' workshops overhanging the river, dates back to 1345. From the terrace in the middle of the bridge, you can look west toward the softly curved arches of the elegant Ponte Santa Trinita. One of the many blown up by the retreating Germans in August 1944, this bridge was carefully reconstructed, exactly as Ammannati had built it in the 16th century.

The Via Por Santa Maria runs from the Ponte Vecchio toward the Duomo. One of Florence's busiest shopping streets, it leads to the **Mercato Nuovo** (New Market), housed beneath a 16th-century loggia. The main attraction of the Mercato Nuovo (also known as the Straw Market even though straw products haven't been sold here in decades) are the stalls selling bags, small leather goods, and assorted souvenirs. Look for the 17th-century bronze statue of a boar, a copy of the much loved *Il Porcellino* (the little boar), on the

Ponte Vecchio—"The Old Bridge"—Florence's oldest and most beloved.

south side. Legend has it that if you stroke his nose and throw a coin into the fountain, you will be sure to return to the city.

Turn right one block north of the market and you will find the unusual church of **Orsanmichele.** The original building was an open-sided loggia, like the Mercato Nuovo, and was re-built in 1337 by the silk guild for use as a market. When it was converted to a church in 1380, the sides were built with Gothic windows (later bricked up), and the two upper stories, added in the early 15th century, were used as an emergency granary (in the rear left-hand corner of the ceiling you can actually see the ducts through which grain was poured into waiting sacks). Mystical and mysterious, the pillared interior is dominated by Orcagna's splendid 14th-century altarpiece, built around a miracle-working icon-like image of the Madonna.

Adopted by the city's wealthy merchant and craft guilds, the plain church's square, fortress-like exterior was embellished with Gothic-style niches and statues during the late 14th and early 15th centuries. Each guild paid for one of the 14 niches and commissioned a statue of its patron or favorite saint.

On the north side of the church (along via dei Lamberti) stands a copy of Donatello's *St. George* (the original stands in the Bargello). Commissioned by the armorers' and swordsmakers' guild, this work was one of the first masterpieces of Renaissance sculpture.

Ghiberti's statues of *St. Matthew* and *St. Stephen* can be seen on the west side of the church, opposite the important 13th-century Palazzo dell'Arte della Lana. Look at the palazzo's impressive upper floors (*Saloni*), reached via an overhead walkway from the church; they were once the headquarters of the powerful wool merchants' guild.

To the east of the palazzo runs Via dei Calzaiuoli, another busy pedestrian street, lined with numerous boutiques, ice-cream shops, and pizza bars, connecting the Piazza della Signoria (to the south) with the Piazza del Duomo (to the north).

SAN LORENZO TO SANTISSIMA ANNUNZIATA

San Lorenzo

The narrow Borgo San Lorenzo begins just north of the Baptistery, and leads into a small square at the foot of the church of **San Lorenzo**. The rough, unfaced stone façade of this church looks for all the world like a huge Tuscan barn. Financed by the Medici, the prestigious project was built by Brunelleschi between 1425 and 1446, with its facade to have been completed by Michelangelo: It never was, but the artist's model is on display at the Casa Buonarotti museum. For once at least, 19th-century architects didn't try to finish the job.

Florence's first entirely Renaissance church and one of Filippo Brunelleschi's earliest architectural triumphs (before he built the Duomo's cupola), the building was begun on the site of a fourth-century basilica. Cosimo Il Vecchio later had his palace built within sight of the church (the Palazzo Medici-Riccardi, with its entrance on Via Cavour). He liked to consider the Church of San Lorenzo as the Medici's parish church.

A door in the left wall of the church leads to the cloister and the stairs up to the **Biblioteca Laurenziana** (Laurentian Library), one of Michelangelo's architectural masterpieces. A monumental staircase climbs to the tranquil reading room, graced with a splendid wooden ceiling and earthy terracotta floor. Commissioned by Pope Clement VII in 1524 to house a precious collection of Medici books and manuscripts, and opened to the public in 1571, it's regarded as one of the most beautiful libraries in the world.

The sober church of San Lorenzo was the burial site of many of the Medici. Cosimo Il Vecchio himself is in the crypt beneath the dome, while his father and mother are in the Old Sacristy, along with his two sons, Piero Il Gottoso and Giovanni, in a sumptuous porphyry and bronze tomb by Verrocchio. That giant of early Renaissance art, Donatello (who decorated the Brunelleshi-designed Old Sacristy), is buried in the left transept.

But San Lorenzo is best known and most visited for the far more sumptuous Medici tombs, found in the **Cappelle Medicee** (Medici Chapels). To visit them, you must go outside and walk around to the opposite end of the church, where you will find the entrance in Piazza Madonna degli

The rough façade of the church of San Lorenzo gives little indication of what awaits the visitor, within.

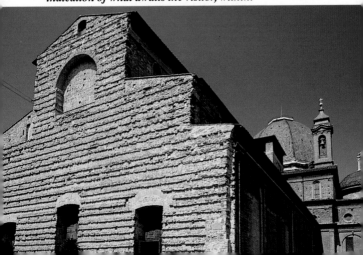

Aldobrandini amidst a jumble of stalls from the daily outdoor tourist market. From the crypt, filled with the tombs of minor family members, a staircase leads up to the **Cappella dei Principi** (the Chapel of the Princes). This early 17th-century Baroque extravaganza (added on after the completion of the New Sacristy; see below) was intended to be the family burial vault to surpass all others. The workmanship of multi-colored inlaid marble and semi-precious stones is astounding, even if by today's standards the over-the-top taste is dubious. Six massive sarcophagi bear the mortal remains of some less known Medici (left to right from the entrance): Cosimo III, Francesco I, Cosimo I, Ferdinando I, Cosimo II, and Ferdinando II.

Follow the stream of visitors to the main attraction, the **New Sacristy** (*Sagrestia Nuova*), reached via a corridor beside the stairs. This is an amazing one-man show by Michelangelo, who spent more than 14 years designing the interior and creating seven of the sculptures. Commissioned in 1520 by the future Pope Clement VII (the illegitimate son of Giuliano de' Medici) as a worthy resting-place for both his father (killed in the Duomo during the Pazzi conspiracy) and uncle (Lorenzo Il Magnifico), it was also to accommodate two recently deceased cousins of the same name (also named Giuliano, Duke of Nemours, and Lorenzo II, Duke of Urbino).

The two more illustrious members of the Medici clan are buried to the right of the entrance, beneath Michelangelo's fine *Virgin and Child*, which is flanked by figures of the Medici patron saints, Cosmas and Damian. But it is the two undistinguished cousins, ironically enough, who have been immortalized by Michelangelo in two of the most famous funeral monuments of all time. On the right stands an idealized, war-like Giuliano, Duke of Nemours above two splendid figures symbolizing *Night* (female) and *Day* (male), reclining on the elegantly curved sarcophagus. The unfinished face of *Day* (on the right), with the visible marks of Michelangelo's chisel, makes the figure all the more remarkable. *Night* is accompanied by the symbols of darkness—an owl, a mask, the moon, and a sack of opium symbolizing sleep.

Opposite, a pensive Lorenzo, Duke of Urbino, sits above *Dawn* (female) and *Dusk* (male). The specially foreshortened effect of the upper windows gives the cupola a feeling of still greater height. The walls behind the altar bear architectural sketches and markings, some of which are attributed to Michelangelo himself. Michelangelo worked on the Sacristy from 1521–1534; it was finished by Vasari in 1556.

Out in the sunshine of the piazza, you can turn right, then immediately left into the busy, leather-scented street market of Via dell'Ariento and visit the late-19th-century covered **Mercato Centrale** for a huge dose of local color.

Or walk in the opposite direction alongside the Church of San Lorenzo toward Via Cavour to the massive **Palazzo Medici-Riccardi** (entrance at corner Via Cavour and Via de' Gori). In 1439, Cosimo Il Vecchio, founder of the Medici dynasty, commissioned Brunelleschi's student Michelozzo to build the first home of the Medici clan, where they would live until 1540 when Cosimo I moved to the Palazzo Vecchio (see page 30) and then to the Palazzo Pitti; today it houses Florence's *Carabinieri-* (police-) guarded Prefecture. Purchase a ticket and climb one floor to the jewel-box family chapel, the *Cappella dei Magi*, to see Benozzo Gozzoli's famous fresco, the *Procession of the Magi*. Painted in 1459–1463, it's a lavish pictorial record in rich, warm colors of everybody who was anybody (including a self-portrait of the light-blue hatted artist; ask the custodian to point him out) in 15th-century Florence, including, of course, the whole Medici clan and their supporters. The chapel, restored in 1992, remains exactly as the Medici knew it. The palazzo's ground-floor museum is often used for special exhibits. Exit the palazzo and turn left, and continue north (away from the Duomo) along the busy thoroughfare of Via Cavour (one of the few still open to traffic) to the Piazza San Marco.

Piazza San Marco

The Dominican church and monastery of San Marco houses one of Florence's most evocative museums: the **Museo di San Marco.** Florentine-born Fra Angelico (1387–1455) lived here as a monk, and most of his finest paintings and frescoes, including the great *Deposition* altarpiece, can be seen in the Pilgrim's Hospice *(Ospizio dei Pellegrini)*, to the right of the entrance. Follow signs to the Small Refectory *(Refettorio)*, decorated with a vivid Ghirlandaio mural of

The David

The young promising Michelangelo had just completed the *Pietà* (now on display in Rome's St. Peter's Basilica) when he was commissioned to do the *David* in 1501, the one masterwork most immediately associated with the master Florentine artist who will forever be considered the Renaissance's most influential force. One detractor, the 19th-century Grand Tourist and drama critic William Hazlitt, described it as "an awkward overgrown actor at one of our minor theaters, without his clothes." Those who come today to stand in quiet awe are more inclined to agree with D.H. Lawrence, who considered it "the genius of Florence." A life-size marble copy stands in front of the Palazzo Vecchio in the Piazza della Signoria, while a bronze replica anchors the hilltop Piazzale Michelangelo where the magical sunset views over Florence are the same to have influenced Florence's most famous son over five hundred years ago.

The Last Supper (a favorite subject for monastery dining halls and one of seven in Florence).

The cloister bell resting placidly in the *Sala della Capitolo* has had a checkered career. Donated by Cosimo de' Medici, it was known as *La Piagnona* (The Great Moaner); the puritanical supporters of Savonarola, at one time a prior here, were nicknamed *I Piagnoni* after it, and it was tolled to alert the monks when the friar's enemies came to arrest him in 1498 (see page 18). For this act of treason, the bell was spitefully condemned to 50 years of exile outside the city, and was whipped through the streets all the way out of town.

Upstairs in the dormitory, you can visit the monks' cells, each one bearing a fresco by Fra Angelico or one of his pupils. His masterpiece, the famous *Annunciation,* is located at the top of the stairs and another version can be found in cell number 3. At the end of the row to the right of the stairs are the two cells (38 and 39) once reserved for Cosimo de' Medici's meditations, and at the farthest end of the dormitory are the quarters of Girolamo Savonarola (see above and page 18), the monastery's fire-and-brimstone prior and sworn enemy of the Medici.

Architect Michelozzo expanded the 13th-century monastery in 1437: His superb colonnaded library leads off the dormitory. Its light and airy interior is used for rotating exhibits.

Galleria dell'Accademia

At the east end of Piazza San Marco is a 14th-century loggia and the entrance to the Accademia di Belle Arti (Fine Arts). Founded by Cosimo I in the 16th century, the school was enlarged in 1784 by an exhibition hall and a collection of Florentine paintings. The **Galleria dell'Accademia** (the entrance is along the Via Ricasoli, south of the loggia). Its small but important collection of 13th–16th-century Florentine School paintings includes tapestries and furniture, including some typical Florentine marriage chests.

The gallery's main attraction is its seven sculptures by Michelangelo, whose standout centerpiece is the 4¹/₂-m (15-ft) *David*, perhaps the most famous piece of sculpture in the Western world. Brought here from the Piazza della Signoria in 1873, it is displayed in a purpose-built domed room. Commissioned in 1501 as a symbol of Florence, upon its completion Michelangelo was just 26 years old. Its balanced and harmonious composition and mastery of technique instantly established it as a masterpiece. The other works here are the four *Prisoners* (a.k.a. the unfinished *Slaves*), providing a remarkable illustration of Michelangelo's technique as they emerge from the rough stone. He claimed that all his sculptures already existed within the block of marble, and that he only had to release them. These figures, apparently struggling to break out of the rough marble which hold them as prisoners, offer a wonderful expression of his philosophy.

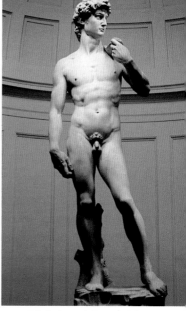

Michelangelo's "David" stands proudly on display at the Galleria dell'Accademia.

The Piazza della Santissima Annunziata uses proportions from the ancient Greeks to achieve a classical grace.

Piazza della Santissima Annunziata

From the Piazza San Marco, a walk along Via C. Battisti leads to the Piazza della Santissima Annunziata, Florence's prettiest square and perhaps the finest example of Renaissance architecture (and proportion) in the city.

The piazza, with graceful colonnades on three sides, was probably designed by Brunelleschi when he built the square's Spedale degli Innocenti (see page 48) in the early 1440s. On the north side, the church of **Santissima Annunziata** was completed in 1481. The architect, Michelozzo, conformed to Brunelleschi's original vision, ensuring the piazza's lasting harmony. The two 17th-century fountains by Tacca, and Giambologna's equestrian statue of Grand Duke Ferdinando I add to the square's feeling of spaciousness.

The church entrance leads into an atrium decorated with frescoes by Andrea del Sarto and others, from which a large door gives access to the extravagantly decorated interior. Immediately left of the entrance, the 15th-century shrine of the *Annunziata* shelters an old painting of the Annunciation, displayed only on special feast days and said to have been painted by a monk with the help of an angel. Reputed to have miraculous properties, it has been the object of pilgrimages and offerings for centuries (shown by appointment only, together with the chapel and tomb of Cellini).

This is known to be the Florentines' favorite church and if you want to peek in on a Florentine wedding, you're most likely to find one here.

The **Galleria dello Spedale degli Innocenti,** on the east side of the square, exhibits 15th- and 16th-century sculptures and paintings belonging to Florence's foundling hospital (*Spedale degli Innocenti* means "Hospital of the Innocents"). Built to Brunelleschi's design in the 1440s, it was the first foundling hospital in Europe. Note the 15th-century glazed terracotta roundels of swaddled babes by Andrea della Robbia on the arched façade—these are the "della Robbia babies" that so appealed to Lucy Honeychurch, the heroine of E.M. Forster's novel, *A Room With A View*. Under the northern end of the colonnade is the small door where abandoned babies were left.

The archway to the left/north of the Spedale leads out of the piazza and to the Via della Colonna and the **Museo Archeologico,** housed in what was once the palace of a grand duke and boasting important collections of ancient Egyptian, Greek, and Etruscan art. The superbly reconstructed Etruscan tombs in the gardens were damaged in the 1966 flood but are since restored.

SANTA MARIA NOVELLA TO SANTA CROCE

The first view of Florence for travelers emerging from the railway station is the slender campanile of Santa Maria Novella rising across the square. This is only the back view of one of Florence's greatest monastic churches; to appreciate the beauty of its multi-colored marble façade you must walk around into Piazza Santa Maria Novella.

The cavernous church of **Santa Maria Novella** was designed by Dominican architects in the mid-13th century, and a small Dominican community still resides within its walls. The upper part of the bold, inlaid marble front was completed in 1470 in Renaissance style by the architect Leon Battista Alberti, who was also responsible for the graceful Palazzo Rucellai nearby. (The lower Gothic facade is a century older.) One of the few Florentine churches the Medici didn't pay for, Santa Maria Novella was funded by the Rucellai family; they had their name put up in large Roman letters under the top cornice, and had the family emblem of a billowing sail repeated along the frieze to make sure their generosity wouldn't go unnoticed.

Walk beneath the soaring vaults of the 100-m- (328-ft-) tall nave to the cluster of richly frescoed family chapels sur-

Some of the magnificent frescoes that grace the walls at Santa Croce date as far back as the 14th century.

rounding the altar. The chancel is decorated with a dazzling fresco cycle by Ghirlandaio depicting *Scenes from the Lives of the Virgin and St. John*, which were paid for by the wealthy Tornabuoni family. Ghirlandaio, Florence's leading "social" painter of the late 15th century, peopled his Biblical frescoes with members of the Tornabuoni clan—one of whom was the mother of Lorenzo Il Magnifico—all dressed in the latest everyday fashions.

To the right of the altar is the **Filippo Strozzi Chapel,** colorfully frescoed by Filippino Lippi, son of the painter Fra Filippo, and the **Bardi Chapel,** with 14th-century frescoes. **The Gondi Chapel** to the left of the altar contains a Brunelleschi crucifix (his reply to Donatello's "peasant" crucifix in Santa Croce; see page 78); it is his only work in wood. On the extreme left is the **Strozzi Chapel,** with 14th-century frescoes of *The Last Judgement, Heaven,* and *Hell* —its benefactors, of course, are depicted in Heaven.

The church's most striking work is Masaccio's *Trinity* (c.1427)—at press time, being restored—on the wall of the left aisle. Famous for the first such handling of early perspective and a convincing illusion of depth, the fresco depicts the crucifixion in a purely Renaissance architectural setting, dramatically breaking from the established canons of religious art.

To the left of the church lies what remains of the monastery, part of which is taken over by the Carabinieri and closed to the public. Exit the church for the separate entrance to the great 14th-century cloister with its three giant cypresses. Known as the **Chiostro Verde** (green cloister) after the greenish tint of the frescoes of the **Universal Deluge** by Paolo Uccello (see page 24), it is flanked by the Refectory (where some detached surviving frescoes are now preserved); a smaller cloister; and the famous **Cappellone degli**

Spagnoli (Spanish Chapel), an impressive, vaulted chapter-house named in honor of Cosimo I's Spanish wife, Eleonora of Toledo. Gigantic 14th-century frescoes by the little known Andrea da Firenze cover its four walls. The artist incorporated a picture of the Duomo complete with its cupola—60 years before it was actually completed.

From the opposite end of the Piazza Santa Maria Novella (note the stone obelisks supported by Giambologna's bronze turtles which marked the boundaries of horse races and chicken races common from approximately 1550 to 1850), the Via dei Fossi—lined with antiques stores—leads down to the riverside Piazza Goldoni. At the small piazza, turn right along Borgognissanti (which also appears as Borgo Ognissanti) to visit the church of **Ognissanti** (All Saints). Contrary to the impression imported by its fine 17th-century façade, and the della Robbia glazed-terracotta relief over the doorway, the church dates from around 1250. Its builders, the *Umiliati* ("Humble Ones"), were a monastic community who, ironically, ran a remarkably lucrative wool business and were among the first to put Florence on the road to financial prosperity. The church contains Botticelli's *St. Augustine*, and in the refectory, Ghirlandaio's other famous *The Last Supper* (*Cenacolo*), both commissioned by the wealthy Vespucci family (famous for the navigator and cartographer, Amerigo, who lent his name to the New World), several of whose members are buried here, as is Botticelli himself.

From the Ognissanti Church, turn left (in the direction from which you came), and follow the narrow Via della Vigna Nuova toward the town center, past the elegant façade of the Palazzo Rucellai. Cross the tony Via Tornabuoni, "Florence's Fifth Avenue," and ahead, on the right, you will see the massive walls of the **Palazzo Strozzi**, begun in 1489 as a private residence. Wrought-iron torch holders and rings for tethering horses are set in the masonry, but the cornice above the street remains unfinished (along with other details) since money for construction ran out after the death of Filippo Strozzi.

The Great Names of Florentine Art

Giovanni Cimabue (1240–1302) moved from the Byzantine tradition to found the Florentine school of painting, but it was the naturalism of his student Giotto (1266–1337) that made Florence the first city of Italian art.

The Early Renaissance was ushered in by Masaccio (1401–1428), with his solid modeled human figures, followed by Andrea del Castagno (1423–1457); Paolo Uccello (1397–1475), master of perspective; and the melancholic Filippo Lippi (1406–1469). In the realm of religious art, the outstanding painters were the friar Fra Angelico (1387–1455), noted for his purity of line and color; Andrea Verrocchio (1435–1488), Leonardo da Vinci's teacher and a fine sculptor; Domenico Ghirlandaio (1449–1494), famous for his frescoes; the exquisitely lyrical Botticelli (1444–1510); and Filippino Lippi (1457–1504), son of Filippo.

Art reached new heights in the early-16th century with artist and scientist Leonardo da Vinci (1452–1519), Michelangelo (1475–1564)—sculptor, architect, painter, and poet—and Raphael (1483–1520). These three master artists epitomized the period known as the High Renaissance.

The great names of Florentine architecture were Giotto, Filippo Brunelleschi (1377–1446), his student Michelozzo (1396–1472), and Alberti (1404–72). The leading sculptors were Lorenzo Ghiberti (1378–1455), creator of the famous bronze doors on the Baptistery; Donatello (1386–1466), perhaps the greatest Early Renaissance sculptor; Luca della Robbia (1400–1482), who specialized in brightly colored, glazed terracotta; and Benvenuto Cellini (1500–1571), who also excelled as a goldsmith.

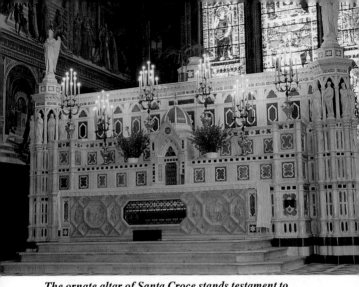

*The ornate altar of Santa Croce stands testament to
Florence's historic marriage of religion and art.*

Head right and toward the Arno, down the boutique-lined
Via dei Tornabuoni to the Piazza Santa Trinita, with its marble Column of Justice—a granite pillar taken from the Baths
of Caracalla in Rome. It was erected by the Grand Duke
Cosimo de' Medici to celebrate his victory over a band of
exiled Florentines anxious to overthrow him and re-establish
a more democratic government.

On the right (west) side of the piazza is the fine 16th-
century façade of the church of **Santa Trinita** by Bernardo
Buontalenti. The Gothic interior comes as a complete surprise. It was built between the 13th and 15th centuries on the
site of an older Romanesque church, the remains of which
are still visible. Look for the late-15th-century Sassetti

Chapel (second on the right from the chancel), with scenes from the life of St. Francis by Ghirlandaio.

The wealthy Strozzi, Davanzati, and Gianfigliazzi families lived in the area, sponsoring richly frescoed chapels. So did the Bartolini-Salimbeni family, whose exquisite, early 16th-century palazzo faces the church. The affluent Spini family built the 13th-century fortress-like residence that stands at the corner of the piazza. Unofficially renamed the Palazzo Ferragamo, after the local family whose expanding empire of fashion and style is located within the palazzo, its street level retail store is one of the area's most alluring.

In the **Palazzo Davanzati** (closed since 1995 for restoration but expected to reopen in 2001) you can see how wealthy medieval and Renaissance Florentines once lived. Although this 14th-century palace presents a stern exterior, the rooms within are full of color. Everything, including toilets and kitchens, has been preserved in period style: Notice the lovely, lavish *trompe l'œil* frescoes in the Sala dei Pappagalli.

Beyond the palazzo (the general Post Office) on the left is the colonnaded Via Pellicceria, which leads to the grand **Piazza della Repubblica.** A jumble of medieval buildings was cleared during the 19th century to create Florence's central square, which occupies the site of the original Roman forum of Florentia. Its stylish cafés fill up at lunchtime with office workers from the surrounding banks and businesses and there's usually live music on summertime evenings.

Turn right (south) at the far side of the square. At the Mercato Nuovo, turn left along Via Porta Rossa, which changes names (Via della Condotta) until you emerge into the **Piazza San Firenze.** This small square is dominated by the towering Baroque façade (unusual in a most un-Baroque city) of San Firenze, the seat of Florence's Law Courts.

Take the narrow Borgo dei Greci on the south side of Piazza San Firenze, heading east until its intersection with Via Bentaccordi. This is one of the few curved streets in medieval Florence, and it owes its shape to the fact that it once ran round the outside of Florence's Roman amphitheater. Follow it around to the left until you emerge into the open space of Piazza Santa Croce.

Piazza Santa Croce

In what is a mostly residential neighborhood today, the vast expanse of **Piazza Santa Croce** formed one of the social and political hubs of Renaissance Florence. Lorenzo and Giuliano de' Medici used to stage lavish jousts here, and defiant Florentines turned out in force during the 1530 siege to watch or take part in their traditional football game (reenacted here every summer; see Calendar of Events, page 90). The buildings on the right-hand side of the square, with their cantilevered upper floors, were typical of the late medieval city.

The cavernous Franciscan church of **Santa Croce** started off in 1210 as a modest chapel, situated—in true Franciscan tradition—in the middle of a working-class district. Arnolfo di Cambio, the architect of the Palazzo Vecchio and the Duomo, drew up the plans for a larger church, which was completed in the 14th century. The interior, beneath its open roof-beams, is grandly Gothic, while the style of the façade is 19th-century Neo-Gothic.

The church is the last resting place of some of the most illustrious figures in Italian history, many of them born in Tuscany. Just inside the door on the right is the **tomb of Michelangelo,** designed by his first biographer, the 16th century artist and architect Giorgio Vasari. Though Michelangelo died in Rome, his body was brought back to Florence for the finest funeral in Florentine memory. The seated figures on the monument represent, from left to right, Painting, Sculpture, and Architecture — the three realms of art in which he remains immortal.

The next tomb on the right wall, that of Florentine Dante Alighieri, lies empty, much to the dismay of Florence (he was exiled for political reasons). His body lies in Ravenna, where he died; the city has never given in to Florentine pleas for its return (a statue to him stands just outside Santa Croce's main entrance). Farther along is the tomb of Niccolo Machiavelli (1469–1527), civil servant, political theorist, historian, and playwright (his famous book *The Prince*—which gives advice on how to rule a state—has made his name,

Stop in at Santa Croce and pay a visit to the tomb of the incomparable Michelangelo.

fairly or not, synonymous with the ruthless pursuit of power). Gioacchino Rossini (1792–1868), Florentine by adoption and the composer of *The Barber of Seville* and *The William Tell Overture*, is also buried here.

Opposite Michelangelo is the tomb of the Pisan genius Galileo Galilei (1564–1642), who is shown holding the telescope, which he invented. A plaque on the front of the tomb depicts the four moons of Jupiter, which he discovered with the use of the instrument. On the same side of the church, beside the fourth column from the door, lies sculptor Lorenzo Ghiberti, creator of the famous Baptistery doors (see page 25) among other masterworks. Step gingerly over many 13th- and 14th-century tomb slabs set in the floor, their effigies badly worn but still visible.

A tranquil chapel in the left transept houses a colored wooden Christ on the cross carved by Donatello. His friend Brunelleschi mockingly dismissed the sculpture as "a peasant on the cross" (Brunelleschi's answer can be found hanging in the Church of Santa Maria Novella).

The honeycomb of family chapels on either side of the high altar contains a wealth of frescoes dating from the 14th to 16th centuries. To the right of the altar, in the **Bardi Chapel,** you'll find Giotto's finest and arguably most moving works—scenes from the life of St. Francis, painted around 1320.

The adjoining chapel, containing Giotto frescoes of the life of St. John, were commissioned by the Peruzzi—rich bankers who donated most of the money for the church's imposing sacristy where a fragment of S. Francesco's tunic is displayed.

By a separate outdoor entrance to the right of the church is the **Museo dell' Opera di Santa Croce.** A gravel path leads to the **Cappella dei Pazzi.** The once-

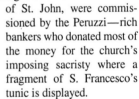

Beside the Church of Santa Croce, the Capella dei Pazzi is a small, but proud, chapel.

tarnished reputation of the Pazzi family (resulting from the assassination of Giuliano Medici in the Duomo) is more than redeemed by this small exquisite chapel. One of the earliest and most important Renaissance religious interiors, it was designed for the Pazzi family by Brunelleschi in 1443, and contains his glazed-terracotta decorations of the Four Evangelists and the tondos of the 12 Apostles by Luca della Robbia.

The former refectory houses a small museum containing frescoes and statues that were removed from the church for preservation, but its greatest treasure is Cimabue's massive 13th-century painted crucifix. Restored after near-destruction by the 1966 flood, it hangs by heavy cables that can raise it out of harm's way by the push of a button, should another flood occur. Outside the museum, beneath the colonnade, is a memorial to Florence Nightingale, who was born in Florence in 1820 and named after the city; she would later find her fame as a nurse in the Crimean War.

There are two more interesting museums close to Santa Croce. The **Casa Buonarroti,** at Via Ghibellina 70, was bought by Michelangelo with intentions of leaving it to his heirs. He lived for a short period of time in one of three small houses eventually combined to create this current residence. It contains letters, drawings, and portraits of the great man, as well as a collection of 17th-century historical paintings illustrating his long and productive life. The exhibits include his famous sculptured relief, the *Madonna of the Staircase*, completed before the artist was 16. His astonishing *Battle of Lapiths and Centaurs* dates from around the same time. You will also find the actual oxen cart used to transport *David* from his studio to Piazza Signoria, its first location.

The **Museo della Fondazione Horne,** situated near the river at Via de' Benci 6, is a superb little 15th-century palazzo, restored, briefly lived in, and eventually bequeathed to Florence in 1916 by Englishman H.P. Horne. On display inside is his priceless collection of paintings, drawings, sculptures, ceramics, furniture, coins and medals, and old household utensils.

THE OLTRARNO

The district on the south bank of the river, called the Oltrarno ("beyond the Arno"), contains some of Florence's most char-acterful neighborhoods. To get there, cross the river at the Ponte alla Carraia (two bridges west of Ponte Vecchio), turn right on Borgo San Frediano, then left into the Piazza del Carmine. The unpretentious church of **Santa Maria del Carmine** houses some of the Renaissance's most seminal frescoes. A young Masaccio and his teacher Masolino, com-missioned by the wealthy merchant Felice Brancacci, worked from 1425 to 1427 on the decorations for the **Brancacci Chapel** at the end of the right transept. Masolino's own work

---

The Medici Arms

Students of heraldry will be busy in Florence, for the coats of arms of wealthy families, trade guilds, and sponsors em-bellish the façades of many palaces, towers, and churches.

The most famous, of course, are the ubiquitous arms of the Medici family, with their six balls, which appear fre-quently. The balls are said to represent pills, for the Medici, whose name means "doctors," were originally members of the guild of spice merchants and apothecaries; they later made their fame and fortune in textiles and banking. Five balls are colored red, but the top ball is blue and bears the golden lily of France—a gift from Louis XI of France in the 15th century.

---

is striking enough, but Masaccio's *The Tribute Money* and the *Expulsion of Adam and Eve from the Garden of Eden* raised the art of painting to an unprecedented level. His feeling for light and space, his dramatic stage-set figures, and the solidity of their forms were considered little short of an inspired miracle. Nothing like them had been painted before; the Renaissance had arrived. Sadly, Masaccio died at the age of 27. It is said that Florentine artists young and old (stories recount visits by Michelangelo and Leonardo who sat and sketched) made pilgrimages to the church to marvel at and learn from Masaccio's achievement. A devastating fire in 1771 somehow left the Brancacci frescoes in tact, but elsewhere in the church you will see the late baroque architecture and styling used to recreate the church. Opposite the Brancacci Chapel is the Corsini Chapel, a rare jewel of the Florentine Baroque style.

As you exit the church, turn right and follow Via Santa Monica and Via Sant' Agostino to the attractive **Piazza Santo Spirito,** attractive for its morning market stalls and the sidewalk cafés that line the tree-lined square. The modest pale-golden façade rising above the back of the piazza is the church of **Santo Spirito.** A monastic foundation of the Augustinian order dating back to the 13th century, the present church was designed by Brunelleschi and built in the second half of the 15th century. The bare, unfinished exterior conceals a masterpiece of Renaissance architectural harmony. The interior's walls are lined with 39 elegant side altars, while slender, gray, stone columns with Corinthian capitals, along with an interplay of arches and vaulted aisles, create an impression of tremendous space.

On leaving Piazza Santo Spirito, head east across the Via Maggio (an important venue of museum-quality antiques stores) in the direction of the Palazzo Pitti.

☛ Palazzo Pitti

This huge palace was built as a symbol of wealth and power by the Florentine merchant Luca Pitti, who wanted to impress his longtime rivals, the Medici. It was begun in 1457, but was continuously enlarged until the 19th century. Pitti died (together with his savings) in 1472, but the Medici were sufficiently impressed by his palace to buy it in 1549, enlarging it substantially, after which it served as the official residence of the Medici (beginning with Cosimo I and his wife Eleonora of Toledo) and the successive ruling families of Florence until 1919, when it was bequeathed to the country. The palace and grounds contain seven museums and galleries (which, with the exception of the principal Galleria Palatina, open and close for renovation far too frequently), plus ornate Italian gardens on the hills behind it—a favorite picnic site.

Visiting the numerous museums housed within the Palazzo Pitti can easily stretch into a full day of sightseeing.

The sumptuous **Galleria Palatina** preserves the magnificent art collection of the Medici and Lorraine grand-dukes, just as the owners hung them—a jigsaw puzzle according to theme and personal preference rather than historical sequence. Priceless paintings decorate 26 dazzling rooms, hung four-high amid lavish gilded, stuccoed, and frescoed decoration. It is the largest and most important collection of paintings in Florence after the Uffizi.

There are superb works by masters such as Titian, Rubens, Raphael, Botticelli, Velázquez, and Murillo, exhibited in grandiose halls adorned with ceiling paintings of Classical themes (the Hall of Mars, Hall of Venus, Hall of the Iliad).

The best of 19th- and 20th-century Italian art can be seen in the interesting **Galleria d'Arte Moderna** (Gallery of Modern Art), on the floor above the Palatina. Here you can discover the exciting works of Tuscany's own Impressionist movement, the *Macchiaioli* (or blotch-painters) of the 1860s. In 1999, one hundred new paintings were added to the already fascinating collection.

Sixteen sumptuous rooms comprise the **Museo degli Argenti** (Silverware Museum), where you can admire some of the Medici's most cherished jewelry, gold, silver, cameos, crystal, ivory, furniture, and porcelain, including Lorenzo Il Magnifico's priceless collection of 16 exquisite antique vases. The room in which they are displayed is the biggest surprise of all, with 17th-century frescoes that create a dizzying optical illusion of extra height and depth.

Also inside the palace is the **Museo del Costume**. Re-opened in 2000 after a complete overhaul, the museum showcases fashions from the 18th century to the present day.

Once you've seen the galleries, take a relaxing stroll in the delightful **Giardino di Boboli,** an Italian pleasure-garden of arbors and cypress-lined avenues dotted with graceful statuary, lodges, grottoes, and fountains.

The entrance to the gardens, at the back of the palace courtyard, leads to the amphitheater, which has a fine view of the palace and the city beyond. Up the hill behind it are the Vasca del Nettuno (Neptune Fountain) and the Casino del Cavaliere, housing the **Museo delle Porcellane,** a fine porcelain collection which is closed more frequently than it is open. Away to the right, at the end of a long cypress avenue, is the unique Piazzale dell'Isolotto, an idyllic island of greenery, fountains, and sculpture set in an ornamental pond; to the left is the coffee shop, most enjoyable for its view of Florence. Returning downhill, head right below the amphitheater to see the **Grotta Grande** or **Grotta dei Musei,** a man-made cave designed by Buontalenti, as well as the much-photographed statue of Cosimo I's court jester, a pot-bellied dwarf, riding on the back of a turtle.

☛ San Miniato al Monte

The church of San Miniato, arguably the most beautiful in Florence and most beloved by Florentines, enjoys a magnificent hilltop location. The easy way to get here is to take a number 12 or 13 bus to Piazzale Michelangelo, but a more interesting alternative is to walk along the ancient city walls or up through the Boboli Gardens.

From the Palazzo Pitti, return to Ponte Vecchio and turn right along the Via dei Bardi. Where the buildings on the left end, allowing a view of the river, you will see an archway in the corner on the right. Go through the arch and follow the Costa dei Magnoli up a steep hill to the **Forte di Belvedere.** This 16th-century fortification offers a panoramic view over the city; its terraces known as "Florence's balcony" are used for rotating exhibits of different themes.

Yet to carve a niche in the international conscience, artists earnestly peddle their work in Piazzale Michelangelo.

Take the road that runs along the foot of the old city wall. Where it drops down to the gateway of Porta San Miniato, turn right instead and follow the narrow road and the steps above it to the main road. Continue along to the right until you find the stairs leading up to **San Miniato al Monte.**

St. Minias, an early Christian martyred in the third century A.D., is said to have carried his own severed head up to this hilltop and set it down on the spot where the church was later built. Easily overlooked if you're short of time, San Miniato is nonetheless one of the city's most romantic and oldest churches and offers a chance to escape to the shady hilltops above the Palazzo Pitti.

Rebuilt in the early 11th century, it is a remarkable example of Florentine-style Romanesque architecture. The

Enjoy an al fresco concert and breathtaking vantage point from the Belvedere Fortress above the Boboli Gardens.

superb green-and-white marble façade, visible from Florence below, contains a 13th-century mosaic representing Christ flanked by St. Minias and the Virgin Mary.

The cool, mystical interior has all the splendor of a Byzantine basilica, with its wealth of richly inlaid marble and mosaic decorations. Note the painted wooden ceiling, and the nave's 13th-century oriental carpet-like marble pavement. Try your best to be here in the late afternoon to hear the Gregorian **vespers** at 5:30pm and mass at 6pm (4:30 and 5pm, respectively, in the winter) by the few remaining monks still in residence.

A small adjoining shop and bar run by the resident Benedictine order offers everything from honey and herb liqueurs to a postcard or a cold drink. Beside the church, the **Cimetero Monumentale delle Porte Sante** dates back to 1864, when burials in the historic center of Florence were banned. Look for the tomb of Tuscan-born Carlo Collodi (née Lorenzini), the author of Pinocchio.

DAY TRIPS FROM FLORENCE

Many travel agencies offer a wide range of guided coach tours, though independent travel to nearby cities is easy enough. Regional bus services (see page 123) cover the whole of Tuscany (orange buses are only useful for shorter excursions within the city's periphery). Here are a few ideas for places that can be reached from Florence in an hour or less by car or public transport.

A winding road climbs for some 8 km (5 miles) through the outlying neighborhoods north of Florence to the charming little hilltop town of **Fiesole** (take the number 7 bus from Santa Maria Novella train station or Piazza San Marco). An ancient Etruscan stronghold and later a Roman settlement, it provides an escape from the city's summer heat, and offers wonderful views over Florence and the Arno Valley.

The bus drops you in the central Piazza Mino da Fiesole, which has a market on Saturdays and a couple of pleasant open-air cafés. Opposite the bus stop is Fiesole's cathedral. Founded in 1028 and completed during the 13th and 14th centuries, **San Romolo** was totally restored in the 19th century, leaving it with a rather drab exterior. Its campanile, visible for miles around, dates back to 1213. A Byzantine atmosphere pervades the interior, which contains the Capella Salutati, with two works by Mino da Fiesole—a tabernacle showing the Virgin with Saints, and the tomb of Bishop Salutati.

To the right of the cathedral is the arched entrance to the **Roman theatre** and its adjacent archaeological site (**Zona**

This convent is a peaceful place for the nuns of San Francesco to uphold their vows.

Archeologico) with the new tourist information office nearby. The well-preserved theater dates from around 100 B.C. and seats some 2,500 spectators. Half original and half restored, it is still used today for performances of plays and music during the popular *Estate Fiesolana* (Summer Festival; see page 90). Below the theater are the remains of Roman baths and a temple. A small but interesting archaeological museum is housed in a replica of the temple just inside the entrance.

From the square, follow the signs for the extremely steep but picturesque **Via di San Francesco** uphill to the church of **San Francesco** and its tiny monastery. The views of Florence from the terrace below the church are gorgeous, and the monastery (and its quirky, free museum of antiquities), with its peaceful little cloisters, is enchanting. A wooded park offers a choice of footpaths back down the hill (Fiesole is crossed by a number of good footpaths for hillside walks—the tourist office has a detailed walker's map).

Rather than take the bus back to Florence, you might enjoy a pleasant walk downhill to the Mugnone valley and into town—allow two hours to return to Florence's center. From the bottom end of the Piazza Mino da Fiesole, head down the main road but immediately fork right down the very steep **Via Vecchia Fiesolana,** the original road to the town. It zigzags down the hillside between centuries-old villas and ancient stone walls, with breathtaking views of Florence to be glimpsed between the cypresses.

You rejoin the main road at the 15th-century Dominican church and monastery of **San Domenico.** This is where Fra Angelico took his vows; his fine fresco of *The Crucifixion* adorns the Chapter House. Just before the church, a right turn at the traffic lights leads to the **Badia Fiesolana** (five minutes away), which served as Fiesole's cathedral until 1028. Rebuilt at the behest of Cosimo Il Vecchio in the 15th century, it is a gem of Renaissance architecture, and often hosts summertime concerts.

Immediately beyond San Domenico, fork right on the tree-shaded Via Giovanni Boccaccio, which winds down gently to the small River Mugnone, and on into the suburbs of Florence. Where the riverbank path ends, cross the bridge and turn right, and you will soon find yourself in the Piazza delle Cure, from which a number 1 or 7 bus (or another half-hour's walk) will return you to the city center.

Pisa

Roughly 80 km (50 miles) west of Florence lies Pisa, the birthplace of Galileo, and home of the fabled Leaning Tower. The

Lean on in to get a better look—Pisa's famous 12th century bell-tower looks as if it could topple at any time.

city was a flourishing commercial center and port during the Middle Ages, until the silting up of the Arno estuary left it stranded—7 miles inland from the coast. The most conspicuous legacy of Pisa's wealthy and powerful past, and what everybody comes to admire, are the architectural wonders of the **Campo dei Miracoli** (Field of Miracles, a.k.a. Piazza Duomo) —the Duomo, the Battistero, and, of course, the cathedral's circular campanile, the Leaning Tower.

Built during Pisa's Golden Age, the centerpiece of the grassy Field of Miracles is the white marble **Duomo,** the most important and influential Romanesque building in Tuscany, and the first to use the much-copied horizontal "banding" of gray-and-white marble stripes. It was begun around 1063 and completed by the 13th century (its beautiful bronze doors facing the tower date from 1180). The striped decoration is repeated in the vast interior, which also boasts an ornate wooden ceiling. The cathedral's masterpiece, however, is undoubtedly the magnificent carved pulpit by the local Giovanni Pisano (1302–1310). Opposite the pulpit is the 16th century **Galileo Lamp,** whose movement inspired his theory of pendulum movement. The apse's dazzling mosaics depicting **Christ Pantocrator** were finished in 1302 by Cimabue.

The **Battistero** (Baptistery) was started in 1152 but not completed until the 14th century. The sparsely decorated interior, famous for its excellent acoustics, contains a superb hexagonal pulpit carved in 1260 by Nicola Pisano, father of Andrea and Giovanni.

However, it is the world-famous, 57-m (187-ft) **Campanile** of the cathedral, which really captures the eye, just as beautiful and delicate as carved ivory, and now leaning out of true verticalness by 4.5 m (15 ft), though measurements vary. Begun after the Duomo and Baptistry in 1173, it began to lean when only three of the eight stories had been completed, since the shifting ground beneath the Campo is a waterlogged sand—hardly ideal foundation material (the Duomo and Baptistery are also marginally off kilter). Various architects attempted to correct the lean as construction work continued, resulting in a slight bend by the time of the tower's completion in 1372. It has been closed indefinitely since 1990 for preservation work, and recent efforts seem to have stopped its yearly list, but no one expects to see it reopened to the public (even its bells were silenced in 1993 to avoid harm from the vibration). It is beautiful to view from afar nonetheless, especially at night, when the tower is illuminated as if from within.

On the north side of the piazza stretches the walled **Camposanto,** a unique 13th-century, cloister-like cemetery (filled with sacred dirt brought back from the Holy Land), the walls of which were once covered with remarkable 14th- to 15th-century frescoes, some by Benozzo Gozzoli. These were badly damaged during World War II bombing raids, and were removed to the Museo delle Sinopie in Piazza Duomo. The **Museo del Duomo,** housed in a former 13th-century monastery in the Piazza Duomo, shelters a wealth of artwork taken from the Duomo and Baptistry.

This is all testimony to Pisa's heyday as a flourishing seaport colonized by the Greeks, then settled by the Etruscans, and later taken by the Romans. Long desired and fought over as an outlet to the sea by an envious Florence, the city was forcibly taken by Florence in 1406. Yet only 15 years later its harbor lay silted-up and eventually abandoned.

☞ **Siena**

Siena, about 34 km (21 miles) south of Florence, is still a medieval hilltop city, and Florence's most popular and enjoyable excursion. Its walls enclose a maze of narrow, winding streets that have survived virtually unchanged since the 16th century and earlier. It can be reached easily from Florence by SITA's regular and frequent express bus service (see page 124).

As you approach Siena along a road cut through a succession of undulating hills covered with a rich, reddish-brown soil, you'll understand how the Crayola color "burnt sienna" came by its name. The city itself is a wonderful marriage of brick and stone, all weathered reds and warm pinks.

Perennial spectators are in luck — Siena's Piazza del Campo is home to the unique Il Palio horse race.

Imposing Gothic architecture prevails within the city walls, from the main square's early 14th-century Palazzo Pubblico, with its graceful and slender 97-m (320-ft) tower, the Torre del Mangia, to the grand zebra-striped cathedral and many fine palazzi.

The heart of the city is the huge, sloping, fan-shaped **Piazza del Campo** (commonly known as Il Campo), where the exciting Palio horse-race (see page 75) takes place twice each summer, with tickets virtually impossible to obtain. Siena's atmosphere of aristocratic grandeur befits the proud Ghibelline stronghold it once was. According to ancient myth, it was founded by the descendants of Remus (whose twin brother Romulus founded Rome), while in reality it was colonized by the ancient Romans under Augustus. This proudest and most stubbornly independent of Tuscan cities fell under Florentine sway until the year 1555 and, soon thereafter, slipped into a centuries-long slumber.

Within the Campo's **Palazzo Pubblico** is the **Museo Civico,** where you can see Siena-born Simone Martini's early yet

Florentine Men of Letters

Dante Alighieri (1265–1321), member of a Guelph family, was exiled by a faction of his party for the last 19 years of his life. His immortal poetic work, *The Divine Comedy*, describing a journey through Hell and Purgatory to arrive at last in Paradise, is one of the great landmarks of world literature. In it he juxtaposes divinely ordained political and social order with the ugly reality of the corrupt society around him. Dante was the first to write his masterpiece not in the usual scholarly Latin, but in his everyday language, thus establishing the Tuscan vernacular as "pure Italian" spoken today and used as the language of literature.

Petrarch (Francesco Petrarca, 1304–1374), born in Arezzo, was the son of a Florentine lawyer. Poet, scholar, and a lifelong friend of Boccaccio, he was regarded as one of the most learned men of his time, and was instrumental in the rediscovery of Classical literature that laid the basis for the flowering of Renaissance lyric poetry. He is best known for poems to "Laura," in which he expresses an idealized and unrequited love.

Giovanni Boccaccio (1313–1375) was a Classical scholar and university lecturer, specializing in the works of Dante. Survivor of the Black Death, he used his experiences as the basis for his marvelous collection of prose tales, *The Decameron*. Written in an Italian still easily understood, the work is unrivaled for its gentle eroticism, humor, and vivid characterization.

important frescoes of the *Maestà* (Madonna Enthroned; 1315), and the *Condottiere Guidoriccio da Fogliano* (1328) on his richly caparisoned horse. In the next room are local master Ambrogio Lorenzetti's impressive allegorical frescoes, *The Effect of Good and Bad Government* (1339), one of the largest medieval paintings of a secular theme.

Almost all of historic Siena is closed to traffic. Wander freely through the picturesque, winding, and hilly streets to the great Gothic **Duomo.** Perched atop Siena's highest point and begun in 1196, it's visible from afar for its striking black-and-white striped exterior—a motif repeated in the city's coat of arms. The attractions within include the uniquely intricate inlaid marble floor, a splendid sculptured octagonal pulpit (1265) by Nicola Pisano, and Pinturicchio's colorful historical frescoes (1509) in the adjoining Piccolomini Library. In the neighboring Museo dell' Opera del Duomo, the splendid *Maestà* (1308) by local master painter Duccio is the focal point. He is one of the leading Italian painters of Siena's important 13th- and 14th-century school of art, whose finest examples are on display in the city's art gallery, the **Pinacoteca** (housed not far from the Duomo in the imposing Palazzo Buonsignori).

If you're in Italy at the right time of year (July 2 and August 16), it's worth going out of your way to see the **Palio,** a traditional bareback horse-race that has been held in the Piazza del Campo since the 13th century. Through contacts, friends, or sheer will power, try to reserve a seat in the stands or a place on a balcony with a view, as the crush and excitement in the Campo (where no tickets are needed for the huge and very emotional crowd bearing the peak-summer heat) can be, at best, uncomfortable. After a stately hour-long parade of colorful pages, men-at-arms, and knights and flag-twirlers dressed in 15th-century costumes, ten fiercely competitive bareback riders, each representing a different *contrada* (city ward), battle it out during three wild laps around the dirt-covered piazza. The winning contrada is awarded the highly coveted *Palio*—a painted silken standard. The only rule is that the riders must not interfere with each other's reins; otherwise, anything goes—and often does. As you watch this highly charged, sometimes violent spectacle, you'll be transported back to medieval times.

San Gimignano

The walled medieval town of San Gimignano is one of the most evocative and quintessentially picturesque in Italy. Strategically set on a hilltop, its skyline bristles with the

Go back in time in the medieval squares of San Gimignano, and be sure to try the local cuisine.

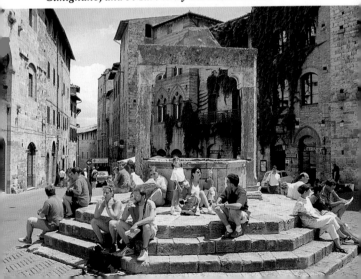

angular outlines of traditional 12th–13th-century Tuscan tower-houses. At one time the town could boast over 70 of them—it was a matter of prestige to build the tallest tower possible. Today, just over a dozen remain, but that's still more than enough to make it the best-preserved (and most popular) medieval town in Tuscany, and to earn it the proud appellation "*delle belle torri*" (of the beautiful towers) and the crowds of tourists that go with it.

Here you can stroll through streets and squares barely changed since Dante arrived as a Florentine envoy in 1300. The plain-façade 12th-century **Collegiata** church (also called the Duomo, though it is not officially a cathedral) is filled with impressive frescoes. Don't miss its tiny **Capella di Santa Fina** (1475), decorated with elegant Ghirlandaio murals depicting San Gimignano's towers in the background. Santa Fina, only 15 years old when she died in 1253, was a local mystic who was adopted as one of the town's patron saints (together with San Gimignano himself).

The center of town life is the 13th to 14th century **Palazzo del Popolo** (Town Hall), with its 36-m (117-ft) tower, the **Torre Grossa** (the only one in town that can be climbed), a superb little courtyard, and unusual frescoes of hunting and courtly love; at the highest point in town is the **Rocca** (citadel), with panoramic views across the countryside. Don't miss the 13th century church of **Sant'Agostino** for its fresco cycle (in the choir) by the 15th century Florentine painter Gozzoli, depicting *Scenes from the Life of St. Augustine*.

In high season, bus tours can seem to overwhelm this small town. But come early, or late, and avoid the crush. And if you have your own wheels, stay on for dinner at one of a handful of good local trattorias known for their rustic but delicious **cucina toscana.**

Churches, Palaces, Museums, and Galleries

All hours listed are subject to change. It is a good idea to consider alternative activities when planning your day. You may want to refer to the following websites: <www.comune.firenze.it> and <www.firenze.turismo.toscana.it>. Also note that ticket sales end 20–60 minutes prior to closing times.

Basilica di Santa Croce, *Piazza Santa Croce*. Giotto frescoes, Donatello's crucifix, tombs of Michelangelo, Machiavelli, Galileo, and others. Open weekdays: 9:30am–5:30pm (summer); 8am–12:30pm and 3–5:30pm (winter); Sun and holidays 3–5:30pm, closed Wed. Free. (See page 56.)

Basilica di San Lorenzo, *Piazza San Lorenzo*. Works by Donatello and Filippo Lippi, Michelangelo's *Biblioteca Laurenziana* next door. Open 7am–noon and 3:30–6:30pm. Admission fee. (See page 41.)

Basilica di San Miniato al Monte, *Via Monte alle Croci*. Florence's oldest, and one of Italy's most beautiful churches, offering panoramic views over the city. Open 8am–noon and 2–7pm (2:30–6pm Nov–Mar). Free. (See page 66.)

Il Battistero, *Piazza San Giovanni* (facing the Duomo). Thirteenth-century mosaics and Ghiberti's famous bronze doors (replicas). Open noon–6:30pm, 8am–1:30pm Sun and holidays. Admission fee. (See page 25.)

Campanile di Giotto, *Piazza del Duomo*. Giotto's fine bell tower for the Duomo, with 400-odd steps to the top (no elevator). Open 8:30am–6:50pm (5pm closing Nov– Mar). Admission fee. (See page 24.)

Cappelle Medicee, *Piazza Madonna degli Aldobrandini.* Tombs of the Medici rulers; Michelangelo sculptures in the New Sacristy. Open 8:15am–5pm (closed most Mondays). Admission fee. (See page 42.)

Duomo (Cattedrale di Santa Maria dei Fiori), *Piazza del Duomo.* Brunelleschi's exquisite cupola. Open weekdays 8:30am–7pm and Sat 8:30am–5pm (first Sat of every month open till 3.20pm only); closed Sun. Admission fee. (See page 22.)

Galleria degli Uffizi, *P.le degli Uffizi,* 6. 13th–18th century Italian and European art, one of the world's most important and prestigious collections. Open Tues–Sun 8:15am–6.50pm, Sat till 10pm in summer; last entry 45 mins before closing); closed Mon. Admission fee. (See page 34.)

Galleria dell'Accademia, *Via Ricasoli,* 60. Michelangelo's *David* and several unfinished sculptures, as well as a variety of Florentine art. Open Tues–Sun 8:15am–6.50pm, Sat till 10pm in summer; last entry 45 mins before closing. Admission fee. (See page 46.)

Museo Archeologico, *Via della Colonna,* 38. Egyptian, Etruscan, Roman, and Greek art. Open Mon 2–7pm, Tues and Thurs 8:30am–7pm, Wed, Fri, Sat 8:30am–2pm. Admission fee. (See page 49.)

Museo dell'Opera del Duomo, *Piazza del Duomo,* 9. Sculpture and religious art from the Duomo. Open Mon–Sat 9:30am–6:30pm; Sun and hols 8am–2pm. Admission fee. (See page 26.)

Museo di San Marco, *Piazza San Marco,* 1. Restored monastery housing the religious paintings of Fra Angelico and others. Open Mon–Fri 8:15am–1.50pm, weekends and hols 8:15am–6.50pm; closed alternate Sundays and Mondays. Admission fee. (See page 45.)

Museo Nazionale del Bargello, *Via del Proconsolo,* 4. Florentine Renaissance sculpture, including works by Michelangelo, Donatello, and Giambologna. Open Tues–Sat 8:15am–1.50pm, also 2nd and 4th Sun of the month and 1st, 3rd and 5th Mon of the month; last entry 45 mins before closing. Admission fee. (See page 28.)

Museo Storico Topografico ("Firenze com'era"). *Via dell'Oriuolo,* 24. The history of "Florentine, as it was." Open 9am–2pm; closed Thurs. Admission fee.

Palazzo Pitti: Piazza Pitti, a 15th-century Medici residence housing the Galleria Palatina, with magnificently decorated 17th-century rooms and superb collection of 16th-century art. Open Tues–Sun 8:15am–6:50pm, Sat till 10pm in summer. Admission fee. Note that the other museums within the Palazzo Pitti charge separately for admission and follow different hours. For the Galleria del Costume, Tel: (055) 2388713, for the Museo delle Porcellane, Tel: (055) 2388709. Giardine di Boboli, open 9am–dusk, closed 1st and last Mon of the month, last entry one hour before closing. (See page 62.)

Palazzo Vecchio, *Piazza della Signoria.* Sumptuously decorated medieval palace and one-time Medici residence, upstairs. Open Tues, Wed, Sat 9am–7pm; Mon, Fri 9am–11pm (summer); Mon–Wed, Sat 9am–7pm, Thurs and Sun 9am–2pm (winter). Admission fee. (See page 30.)

Ponte Vecchio: Dating to 1345, Florence's oldest bridge, lined with goldsmiths' shops, which has survived floods and wars. (See page 38.)

WHAT TO DO

SHOPPING

Since the Middle Ages, Florentines have held craftsmanship in high regard, and the city's elegant shops are famed for the quality of their merchandise, especially jewelry (particularly gold), leather goods, antiques, and fashion. It is one of Italy's best shopping meccas and one that promises good window shopping.

Shop windows compete for your attention along expensive Via dei Tornabuoni and the slightly less chic Via de' Calzaiuoli and Via Roma and their off-shoots. English is understood in the majority of shops in the city center. Tourist and souvenir **markets** (see page 85) are held daily in the sprawling San Lorenzo area, and the less expansive Mercato Nuovo; a local market every Tuesday morning in the Cascine Park is less about souvenir-buying, but offers a colorful insight to Florentine life.

Most shops (and restaurants) close for a period of 7–10 days (minimum) on and around August 15th. Some tourist-oriented stores in the center of Florence remain open for an *orario continuato* (no lunch break), at least during the busy months, and usually choose not to close for the summer break; some also remain open on Saturday afternoons. Only a few open on Sunday, but it makes for a great day for museum going, church visiting, and joining the local Florentines for a traditional giro in centro (an afternoon stroll). Food shops are closed on Wednesdays afternoons (see OPENING HOURS, page 118).

Antiques and reproductions: Antiques shops are clustered around the **Borgognissanti, Via della Vigna Nuova, Via dei Fossi** (and its parallel street Via del Moro) and **Via della**

Colorful Tuscan pottery makes a vibrant accessory that will brighten any home.

Spada, all on the north (Duomo) side of the river; in **Via Maggio** and **Via Santo Spirito** on the opposite bank in the Oltrarno neighborhood. Specializing largely in furniture, paintings, and decorations, none of them are inexpensive. A major international antiques fair is held biennially at the Palazzo Strozzi (September–October) during uneven years only.

Bric-a-brac addicts will find a permanent, modest-sized flea market on **Piazza dei Ciompi** (the market is open daily in high season) with an overspill of shops in the area just behind the market. There is also an interesting antiques market the third full weekend of every month in the fountain park in front of the **Fortezza di Basso** along Viale di Strozzi.

Framed 18th-century prints of Florence are good buys, especially in the shops around **Piazza del Duomo.** You can also look for unframed prints in the **San Lorenzo market.**

Ceramics: Expensive, high-quality table china (the world-known name Richard Ginori originated in Florence and is still produced outside of town); brightly hand-painted ceramics of centuries-old Tuscan patterns and colors. Several great houseware stores in the center carry selections of these regional specialties at reasonable prices.

Fashion: Florentine designers and manufacturers unfurl their fashions for a string of "Pitti" trade shows for men, women, children and homewares, held in Florence twice a year. All the world-renowned Italian houses sell clothing and shoes in their exclusive boutiques at prices only marginally cheaper than they would be at home. More interesting is the selection of designer accessories such as gloves, scarves, belts, and other leathergoods from regional manfucturers for those less label-conscious buyers who can spot quality when they see it.

Gold and silver: Designer gold jewelry is expensive (and almost always 18-karat), but simpler items such as gold (and occasionally silver) charms, chains, earrings are reasonably priced and widely available. Every piece should be stamped, confirming that it is solid gold (ask to see the stamp, as miniscule as it may be). The ultimate place to window-shop is, of course, along the **Ponte Vecchio,** a bridge lined with dazzling centuries-old jewelers' shops, each window more tempting (and densely stocked) than the last.

The work of Florence's unsung silversmiths is invariably beautiful and practical. Look for pill-boxes, napkin rings, photo frames, cruet sets, sugar bowls, and candlesticks.

Inlays and mosaics: The Florentine specialty of *intarsio*, the art of wood or semi-precious stone inlay, was perfected during the Renaissance (some examples can be seen in the Uffizi). The craft still flourishes, and you'll see modern interpretations (and replicas of classic patterns) for sale in **Lungarno Torrigiani, Via Guicciardini,** and **Piazza Santa Croce.** Larger items like table tops are inevitably expensive and exorbitant to ship; small, framed "naïve" pictures of birds, flowers, Tuscan landscapes, or views of Florence are charming mementos, and less expensive.

Leather: Florence has been well-known for its quality leather goods since the Middle Ages. This is the home town of leather greats Ferragamo and Gucci; Prada and Fendi (associated, respectively, with Milan and Rome) are also produced in the Florentine foothills. San Lorenzo's famous market is awash with leather stalls (and the shops hidden behind them) that sell everything from handbags and luggage to wallets and gloves. Shoe shops are traditionally concentrated along **Via dei Calzaiuoli** ("The Street of Cobblers") and Borgo San Lorenzo.

Don't miss the **Leather Guild School** in Santa Croce Church, housed in the adjoining monastery (entrance is through the church, in the far right-hand corner behind the altar). Something of a (centuries-old) tourist trap, you'll see apprentices and professionals cutting, tooling, and stamping traditional motifs on a wide range of leather goods. A tempting selection of their work, from medium range to very nice quality, is for sale.

The best buys in town are small leathergoods: gloves, belts, purses, wallets, and boxes, in all shapes, sizes, and quality and types of leather. Handbags and outerwear can be gorgeous and tempting but are always expensive; less expensive variations can be found, in stores or the **San Lorenzo market,** but you get what you pay for. The give-away prices once commonplace in the 1970s (together with inexpensive Florentine gold) are long gone.

Paper Goods: Florence has been a major center of hand-printing and bookbinding for centuries, a craft resuscitated in the last few decades. Shops sell specialized stationery, and hand-made marbled (also seen as marblized) papers that cover everything from notebooks and albums, to tabletop items such as frames and desk sets. Leather-bound books such as agendas, address books, and journals are beautifully crafted.

Street Markets

The biggest and most popular market is **San Lorenzo,** which caters to both tourists and locals, and sells everything from soccer banners to sunglasses, with an ever growing emphasis on tourist-attracting goods. You'll find clothing (t-shirts, knitwear, and woolen scarves), shoes, and leatherwear, often at reasonable prices but don't expect high-quality goods. Many stalls accept credit cards, almost all take travelers checks, and some might offer to mail purchases to anywhere in the world (think twice about this). At its center, stretching along Via dell' Ariento, is the late-19th-century structure that houses the **Mercato Centrale,** the city's largest and most colorful food market, bulging at the seams with just about everything from the surrounding Tuscan hills, from fresh fruit and vegetables, to meat, fish, and game. It is a must for local color, photo opts, insight to the Florentines' daily life, culinary heritage, and a better understanding of their wheelings and dealings.

The **Mercato Nuovo,** or **Straw Market,** is conveniently located halfway between the Duomo and the Ponte Vecchio. Housed beneath a 16th-century loggia, a score of stalls sells leather bags and other miscellaneous souvenirs — a far less expansive (and less interesting) selection than its big-sister market at San Lorenzo.

Florence's huge Mercato San Lorenzo is sure to have something for everyone.

A daily **flea market** operates in Piazza dei Ciompi, selling the usual mix of forgettable junk and bric-a-brac found in flea markets the world over. A more genuine antiques market is also held in the same spot, and takes place on the last Sunday of each month.

A huge weekly market sets up every Tuesday morning in **Cascine park,** selling all kinds of goods for a far less touristy clientele (little English is spoken). It's especially good for cheap clothes and shoes, as well as live chickens and rabbits whose days are numbered.

ENTERTAINMENT

Whatever the time of year, there's always something interesting going on in Florence. Information on current events can be found on the weekly "what's on" posters throughout the city (and sometimes posted in hotels), and in the useful monthly publication, *Calendar of Events (Evvenimenti),* available from the tourist office. There are also weekly entertainment listings in the weekend editions of the Italian-language *La Nazione* and *La Repubblica* papers. For up-to-the-minute information on all events, and to get tickets to a range of events, contact *Box Office*, Via della Pergola 10r; Tel. (055) 242361 (pay by credit cards, and they'll deliver tickets to your hotel for a nominal fee). Other box offices — the two most popular venues for music, drama, opera, and dance — are: The Teatro Comunale, Corso Italia 16; Tel. (055) 211158; or the Teatro Verdi, Via Ghibellina 101, Tel. (055)212320.

Music and Theater

Concerts are a year-round feature of Florentine cultural life. Special summertime alfresco concerts are held in the **Boboli Gardens,** and organ recitals are presented in historic churches in September and October (sporadically in winter months — remember there's no heat in these churches). During June, July, and August, nearby **Fiesole** (see pages 67) offers the *Estate Fiesolana* festival of concerts, ballet, drama, and film evocatively staged at the restored Roman amphitheater. The Florentine opera season gets underway in December and runs until April, held mostly at the Teatro Comunale; its "off" months are filled with dance and other concerts.

The highlight of the musical year in Florence is the celebrated *Maggio Musicale* (<www.maggiofiorentino.com>, tickets@maggiofiorentino.com) festival (from mid-May to the end of June), one of Italy's principal music festivals. It attracts some of the finest concert, ballet, and operatic performers in the world, thanks in large part to the artistic direction of principal conductor Zubin Mehta.

Cinema and Nightlife

Almost all English language films screened in Florence have been dubbed into Italian. One place that shows movies in English is the small Cinema Astro near Piazza Santa Croce in the tiny Piazza San Simone; another is the Cinema Goldoni on via dei Serragli on Thursday evenings. Note that many cinemas close for several weeks during the summer, replaced by outdoor cinemas located along the Viale or in the cooler hillsides.

Florence has no shortage of bars, discotheques, and clubs, all of which are enlivened by the large population of students (Florence has more than 20 foreign study-abroad programs) and travelers. Again, the place to look for details of live performances, stadium concerts, special film showings, and so on is the "what's on" posters — there's usually one posted in the tourist office with others about town — or the weekend newspapers.

SPORTS

Swimming: You can swim or just sunbathe at Florence's four open-air pools. Ask at your hotel for details. To enjoy a dip in the sea, you'll have to travel to Tuscany's coastal resorts of Viareggio, Forte dei Marmi, Marina di Pisa, or Tirrenia (accessible by train and bus service).

Tennis and golf: There are public tennis courts in the Viale Michelangelo and the Campo di Marte, as well as at the Campi dell'Ugolino, a very good golf (18 holes), tennis, and swimming complex, just south of Florence toward the Chianti hills. The tourist office can supply more details.

Walking: There are endless possibilities for wonderful walks in the rolling green hills that surround the city, in areas around Bellosguardo, Fiesole, the Certosa del Galluzzo monastery, Poggio Imperiale, or the Arcetri observatory (which stands on the very hill from which Galileo gazed at the stars), all within easy reach of Florence but where you'll feel like you're out in the famously beautiful countryside of Tuscany. The tourist office can supply a useful walking maps of the province of Florence.

CHILDREN

The Italians' love of children is legendary, and they are almost guaranteed to

Cyclists take in the dramatic view from the Piazzale Michelangelo.

make a fuss over them in hotels and restaurants, forgiving them any noise or nuisance they might cause.

Younger children quickly tire of museums and galleries, especially in the heat of summer. Intersperse museum visits with ice cream from the center's many *gelaterie*, or visit the pigeons and horse-and-buggies that congregate in the Piazza della Signoria.

Older children might enjoy the climb to the top of the Campanile or the dome in the cathedral (one will do, as they are similar in panorama), if they can tolerate more than 400 steps each (there are no elevators). Consider a visit to one of the more offbeat museums, such as the "Specola" Natural History Museum, Via Romana 17, in the Oltrarno neighborhood; the Anthropology Museum, Via del Proconsolo 12; the Museum of Mineralogy, the Botanical Museum, and the Museum of Geology and Paleontology, Via La Pira 4. The Stibbert Museum is a taxi-ride away, but worth it if your children might be interested in one of Italy's best collections of Italian, European, and some Oriental armor.

One way to keep children amused and parents happy is to have their portrait sketched by any of the artists or caricaturists who set up stalls under the open loggia of the Uffizi. Or visit the antique carousel in Piazza Strozzi from October through June (admission fee).

Particularly good for children is the ***Museo dei Ragazzi*** (Museum for Kids), a scheme that has created interactive learning spaces for youngsters across Florence with the aim of getting them involved in the art and history of the city. There are multimedia stations across the historic center, notably at the Palazzo Vecchio (Piazza della Signoria), in the Museo di Storia della Scienza (Museum of History and Science) and the Museo Stibbert. Highlights include encounters with historical figures such as Galilei and Vasari through lively narrations.

If you're going to be in Florence for more than a few days, take at least one day off from sightseeing, and have a well-deserved **picnic** in the hills around Fiesole (see page 67). You may also want to go to one of the city's swimming pools, or even escape to the coast for the day (see page 88).

CALENDAR OF EVENTS

25 March — Annunciation Day: a small fair in Piazza della Santissima Annunziata.

March/April — Easter Sunday Scoppio del Carro (Explosion of the Cart): An outdoor oxen-drawn cart full of fireworks in Piazza del Duomo is set off by a mechanical dove that travels by wire from the cathedral's high altar at midday mass.

23 May — Ascension Day, Festa del Grillo (Festival of the Cricket): Fair in Cascine Park popular with children. Crickets in tiny cages sold to be set free.

Mid-May through late-June — Maggio Musical (Musical May): Prestigious program of opera, ballet, and concerts throughout the city by local and visiting artists (website <www.maggiofiorentino.com>)

June to September — Estate Fiesolana: Summer festival of music, ballet, and theater in hill-top town of Fiesole.

24 June — Feast of St. John the Baptist, patron saint of Florence celebrated with fireworks. Calcio in Costume: historical rowdy football/soccer game in 16th-century costume in Piazza Santa Croce and elaborate parade that preceeds it.

2 July and 16 August — Palio di Siena: Historic pageant and raucous horse-race in Siena's beautiful Piazza del Campo.

7 September — Festa delle Rificolone (Festival of the Chinese Lanterns): Evening procession with torches and paper lanterns on Ponte San Niccolo and river banks.

EATING OUT

The emphasis in Tuscan cuisine is on straightforward, simply-prepared country *cucina povera* (poor man's fare) — few seasonings, no elaborate sauces, and the full flavor of primary ingredients from the bounty of Tuscany's fertile land. What you see in this morning's market is what you'll find on tonight's menu: a pauper's cooking fit for royalty.

The staples of the Tuscan kitchen are olive oil and bread. The **olive oil** produced in Tuscany is commonly extra virgin and is widely regarded as the finest in the world — dark green in color, with a rich, peppery flavor. Tuscan olive oil is used at varying degrees on everything from soup to salad.

Your first taste of traditional crusty Tuscan **bread** will immediately tell you it contains no salt (and is never, ever, eaten with butter!). This eccentricity persists from the Middle Ages, when salt was a luxury item. Bread is served with every meal, and is a basic ingredient in many dishes.

The *Mercato Centrale* (see page 85) sells the fresh ingredients that form the basis of most Tuscan dishes.

Restaurants

The streets of the historic *centro storico* are packed with cafés and bars where you can buy a beverage, snack, or quick lunch to enjoy standing at the bar or seated, or to take away. Sitting at a table will cost more, while sitting outside can be twice, or even three times, as expensive). Another option is the *tavola calda* (hot table), a self-service café where you can choose from a selection of pre-prepared dishes (these alternatives can be good options for lunch; but those that cater to tourists usually offer mediocre, though convenient, meals).

Restaurants range from the expensive *ristorante* to the slightly more modestly priced family *trattoria*. Cover (*cop-*

Enjoy culinary delights al fresco — outdoor cafés have an unforgettable charm.

erto) and service (*servizio*) charges are almost always included, but if not, leave 10 or 15 percent for the waiter. Many trattorie offer a three-course, fixed-price *menu turistico* (one "course" may be a vegetable side-dish), which is often a good deal, especially at lunchtime for those who don't want full-portioned dishes.

Breakfast (*prima colazione*) is usually included in the price of accommodation, and almost every hotel now offers what they call an American buffet that can consist of basic rolls, juice, and coffee, or a full array of fresh fruit, yogurt, cereal, and homemade pastries. It is served usually between 7:30 and 10am Lunch (*pranzo*, or *colazione*) is served from 12:30 to 2:30pm, though a limited number of places in Florence's center will serve food throughout the entire afternoon: Cafés will always provide something to fill the gaps.

Dinner (*cena*) begins at around 7:30pm, and is traditionally a full-fledged affair of four courses: *antipasto* (appetizer); *primo* (soup, pasta, and occasionally, risotto); *secondo* (meat, game, or fish, usually grilled or roasted, and served unaccompanied); and *dolci* (dessert). *Contorni* (optional side dishes) of vegetables or salad are ordered separately and arrive with the entree.

What to Eat

Antipasti (appetizers): Among the usual, such as *antipasto misto* (a table offering a mixed spread of starters, sometimes "self-service") and *melone con prosciutto* (cantaloupe with thinly sliced, cured

> Enjoy your meal!
> — **Buon appetito!**
> (bwon appeteetoh)

ham) to be eaten during the summer when cantaloupe is in season, look out for Tuscan specialties like *prosciutto con fichi* (prosciutto with fresh figs), *crostini* (toast-rounds topped with either chopped chicken livers, anchovies, capers, etc.), *fettunta* (toasted country bread rubbed with garlic and drizzled with olive oil). This is unfussy farmer's fare and it never disappoints.

Primi (first courses): Traditional Tuscan soups include *pappa al pomodoro* (tomato soup thickened with bread), *ribollita* (a filling "twice boiled" bread-based vegetable soup), and *la minestra* (a seasonal vegetable soup sometimes with pasta).

There are limited but excellent pasta possibilities. Typically Tuscan are *pappardelle alla lepre* (broad noodles, usually homemade, with a tomoato-based sauce of wild hare), as well as *spaghetti*, *penne*, and *strozzipreti* (a "priest strangler" of pasta, cheese, and spinach, usually baked in the oven), dressed in a simple tomato sauce. Some restaurants will serve half portions *(mezza porzione)* of pasta upon request.

First-course non-pasta options are *polenta ai cinghiali* (a kind of cornmeal porridge dressed with a wild boar ragu), *panzanella* (a refreshing summertime salad of bread with tomato, red onion, basil, and cucumber), *risotto ai funghi porcini* (slow-cooked rice with porcini mushrooms), and a specialty of *cacciucco* (a rich fish stew in red wine, tomato, and peppers) that can pass as an entree.

Secondi (second courses): every visitor to Florence ought to try the famous *bistecca alla fiorentina*, a huge, charcoal-grilled T-bone steak, served with lemon or drizzled with olive oil, at least once. Each steak is at least 2 cm (1 inch) thick and weighs 600-800g (21-28 oz), charred and crispy outside, rare and tender inside. It's sold by weight, and is not inexpensive. It is common for two people to share one *bistecca*.

Another classic Florentine main course (not as popular with non-Italians) is *trippa alla fiorentina,* which is tripe, cut into thin strips, gently fried in olive oil with onion.

Also on the menu are *fegato alla fiorentina* (sautéed liver with sage or rosemary), *arista* (roast loin of pork with rosemary and garlic), *fritto misto* (fried chicken, lamb, and rabbit, with vegetables; this plate often includes calves brains), *peposo* (beef stewed in a black pepper and tomato-based sauce), and *stracotto* (tender beef stewed with red wine and tomato).

Chicken turns up on the Tuscan dinner table, but Tuscans love game while in season and they are more inclined to appreciate pigeon (*piccione*), pheasant (*fagiano*), and rabbit (*coniglio*). You will find this game fare roasted (*arrosto*), stewed (*in umido*) or simply grilled (*alla griglia*). Simple preparation is always key in the *cucina toscana*.

A few restaurants specialize in fish and seafood. Fish entrees from Tuscany's port city of Livorno (Longhorn) might include *baccalà alla livornese* (a salted cod, tomato, and garlic-based stew), but will simply follow the market's offerings.

Contorni (side-dishes): In Italy, vegetables *(verdure)* are ordered and charged for separately. Try *carciofini fritti* (fried baby artichokes), or grilled mushrooms such as porcini (*funghi* or *porcini alla griglia*). Typical Tuscan side-dishes are *fagioli all'uccelletto* (boiled white beans sautéed with tomato and sage), *fagioli al fiasco* (same ingredients, but stewed), *fagioli all'olio* (boiled white beans, seasoned with olive oil, salt, and pepper, and eaten room temperature). *Insalata mista* (a side salad) is more interesting than the iceberg variety, but don't expect this to be included with any meal.

Dolci (desserts): Generally, desserts do not hold the same importance they do in some other cuisines. Fresh fruit *(frutta di stagione)* or a fruit salad *(macedonia)* made of fresh fruit and ice cream *(gelato)* are the most common desserts. *Cantuccini* and *biscottini di Prato* (Prato is a town outside of Florence) are hard almond biscuits that you soften by dipping into a glass of *vin santo*, a sweet dessert wine.

Picnics

For a breath of air, make up a picnic lunch and head for the hills of Fiesole, the Boboli Gardens, or the terrace of San Miniato in the area of Piazzale Michelangelo. The only central square providing shade is Santo Spirito near the Pitti Palace. Buy fresh fruit and bread from the market, then find one of the many delicatessens *(pizzicheria* or *salumeria)* or small grocers *(alimentari)* who stock a wide range of food and drink (including mineral water and soft drinks), and often sell sandwich rolls *(panini)*. If you'd like to add wine to your picnic, you may have to purchase it at a separate shop.

Try *finocchiona*, Tuscany's fennel-studded salami, and don't neglect the wide range of Italian hams, salamis, the balogna-like *mortadella,* sausages, and other cold meats.

Cheese is an important picnic ingredient: Try *stracchino*, *pecorino* (a tangy sheep's-milk cheese), *ricotta*, *provola* (smoked or fresh), and *gorgonzola*, *parmigiano,* and

Cooking is essentially regional. Each of the country's 18 regions have their own unique specialties rarely found outside their boundaries, while for similar dishes the terminology may vary. There are at least half a dozen names for octopus or squid.

grana. The younger variety is eaten in chunks, the more aged is grated over pasta.

Beating the Heat

Summer heat in Florence can be overwhelming. Hot afternoons are best occupied by retreating to the shade of a café or *gelateria*.

Thirst-quenchers in Florence range from good Italian beers (*birra*) to summertime iced tea, peach or lemon flavored (*tè freddo alla pesca* or *al limone*), a non-alcoholic bitter (*amaro*), freshly squeezed fruit juices (*spremuta*), and iced espresso (*caffè freddo*). For children there's orangeade or lemonade (*aranciata* or *limonata*), and of course, a bewildering choice of delicious ice creams (*gelati*).

Assorted flavors from whiskey to melon await you in a local ice cream shop.

Wines and Spirits

The traditional wine of Tuscany is **Chianti**, probably the best known of all Italian wines. For many, Italian wine *is* Chianti — a basic pressing made from the San Giovese grape.

After a brief period of dormancy, the Chianti production has experienced a resurgence of popularity and sales, and is once again considered one of Europe's premier wines.

Quality and price vary, but it's generally all of good — sometimes superb — quality. The official, Consortium-designated Chianti region stretches from Florence to Siena, entitling producers there to bear the seal of the *Gallo Nero* (black rooster). Seals with a gold border indicate a *Chianti Classico Riserva* meaning that that vintage was aged a year longer before it was bottled.

Tuscany produces a number of other good, light non-Chianti reds, including *Brolio, Aleatico di Portoferraio* (from the Isle of Elba), *Vino Nobile di Montepulciano* (a stonger full bodied red), and a fine aged red, *Brunello di Montalcino*.

Among the few Tuscan white wines are the excellent dry *Montecarlo*, *Vernaccia di San Gimignano* and the mellow *bianco dell'Elba*.

Consider joining an organized tour of the finest Chianti cellars. The tours take in Tuscany's gorgeous rural scenery, a few attractions on the way, and usually run from July to October (check with tourist information office). Serious wine buffs should contact the Florence-based Custom Tours in Tuscany (in Chicago, Tel. (847) 432-1814; fax (847) 432-1889).

An after-meal espresso (*un caffè*) is also available in decaffeinated form (*decaffinato*). You can order it short, long, *macchiato* ("stained" with a dot of steamed milk), or just *normale*, black. Ordering *cappuccino* after 11am marks you as a tourist, but waiters are accustomed to the request of after-dinner cappucinos by now (ordering coffee together with your dinner remains taboo). For a greater ratio of water with your coffee, order a *caffè americano*.

Tuscans like to end their dining experience with a small glass of *vin santo* ("holy wine"), a deep amber-colored sweet wine. Or choose from a local *grappa* (a distillate of grape must) or *limoncello*, a homemade lemon-infused vodka served ice-cold.

Don't feel compelled to order wine with every meal; there's always the commonplace alternative of mineral water (*acqua minerale*), still or carbonated (*naturale* or *gasata*), or beer. Florence's tap water is heavily chlorinated, but is safe, albeit unpleasant, to drink.

For a comprehensive glossary of wining and dining in Italy, ask at your local bookshop for the *Berlitz European Menu Reader*.

To Help You Order...

Good evening; I'd like a table.	**Buona sera; vorrei un tavolo.**
Good day.	**Buon giorno.**
Do you have a set menu/ tourist menu?	**Avete un menù a prezzo fisso/menù turistico?**
I'd like a/an/some...	**Vorrei...**

beer	**una birra**	meat	**della carne**
bread	**del pane**	milk	**del latte**
napkin	**un tovagliolo**	coffee	**un caffè**
potatoes	**delle patate**	salad	**dell'insalata**
fish	**del pesce**	soup	**una minestra**
fruit	**della frutta**	spoon	**un cucchiaio**
sugar	**dello zucchero**	tea	**un tè**
glass	**un bicchiere**	wine	**del vino**
ice cream	**un gelato**		

...and Read the Menu

manzo	beef	**agnello**	lamb
melanzana	eggplant	**peperoni**	peppers
baccalà	dried cod	**pollo**	chicken
prosciutto	ham	**calamari**	squid
coniglio	rabbit	**fagioli**	beans
sugo	sauce	**sogliola**	sole
formaggio	cheese	**frittata**	omelet
vitello	veal	**uova**	eggs
maiale	pork	**cipolle**	onions

HANDY TRAVEL TIPS

An A–Z Summary of Practical Information

Florence

ACCOMMODATION *(alloggio)* (See also CAMPING, YOUTH HOSTELS, and the list of Recommended Hotels on page 129)
Florence offers a wide range of accommodation, from luxury hotels set in Renaissance palazzi, through more modest hotels, to former *pensioni*. Rental villas (and apartments within villas) are available just outside of Florence for those who intend to rent a car. The following web sites will help with more information: <www.agriturismo.regione.toscana.it>; <www.communicart.it; www.rentvillas.com; www.italianvillas.com>.

Hotels are graded from one to five stars. The Florence Tourist Board (APT) (see also TOURIST INFORMATION OFFICES; <www.firenze.turismo.toscana.it>; e-mail <apt@firenze.turismo.oscana.it>) publishes a list of hotels that details prices and facilities and is updated annually.

During the high season between March and October, Florence becomes very crowded and accommodation is at a premium. Book as far in advance as possible for this period. If you find yourself in Florence without a hotel reservation, head for the Informazioni Turistiche Alberghiere (ITA) office in the Santa Maria Novella railway station (Tel. 055-282893; open daily 8:45am–8pm). For a variable fee (dependent on the classification of the hotel), they will find you a room within your price range.

Florence is expensive, on a par with the major European cities. Prices must be clearly displayed in the reception area and in the rooms. Breakfast (often an abundant buffet but sometimes just rolls and coffee) is almost always included in the room rate but is sometimes optional.

I'd like a single/ double room.	**Vorrei una camera singola/ matrimoniale.**

with bath/shower	**con bagno/doccia**
What's the rate per night?	**Qual è il prezzo per una notte?**

AIRPORTS (*aeroporti*)

The main international airport for Florence is in Pisa. International flights can be seasonal, so check with your travel agent when traveling off season.

Aeroporto Galileo Galilei (<www.safnet.it>; <vespucci@-safnet.it>) is about 81 km (51 miles) west of Florence. Facilities include a self-service restaurant, bar/café, post office, bank, ATM, 24-hour currency-exchange machine, tourist information desk, and car rental desks. For flight information, call (050) 500707 between 7am and 9pm. An hourly train service links the airport with Pisa Centrale (six minutes) and Florence (one hour), between 10:18am–8:25pm. Buy your ticket at the Information Desk at the opposite end of the terminal building from the arrivals area. On your return journey, you can check your bags in at the Air Terminal (Tel. (055) 216073), 7am–5:30pm, at the railway station in Florence.

Florence's own small but growing airport — Aeroporto Amerigo Vespucci — is at Perètola, 5 km (3 miles) northwest of the city. It handles domestic as well as daily flights to and from major European cities. For flight information, call (055) 373498 from 7:30am–11:30pm. To report or check on lost baggage, call (055) 308023. A regular 30-minute bus service (ATAF 62) connects the airport with the SITA bus station in central Florence every 20 minutes; or take a taxi for approximately €15 to midtown destinations.

Could you please take these bags to the bus/train/taxi, please.	**Mi porti queste valige fino all'autobus/ al treno/al taxi, per favore.**
What time does the train for Florence leave?	**A che ora parte il treno per Firenze?**

B

BICYCLE RENTAL *(noleggio biciclette)*
In an effort to reduce congestion and pollution, more and more of the flat **centro storico** is being closed to vehicular traffic. The city has provided bicycles at 17 parking lots (8am–7:30pm) throughout the city and charges a nominal fee to use them for as much time as you like. For better quality bicycles you can try Florence By Bike, via San Zanobi, 120/122r, Tel./fax (055) 488992), where you can also rent scooters. A multi-lingual staff organizes full tours in and out of the city.

C

CAMPING *(campeggio)*
There is only one campsite convenient to the center of Florence, with 240 pitches set on a pleasant hillside above the river east of Piazzale Michelangelo (30 minutes' walk from the Uffizi). Contact Campeggio Italiani e Stranieri (Camping Michelangelo), Viale Michelangelo 80, 50125 Florence; Tel. (055) 6811977, fax (055) 689348. Reservations required.

There are several other campsites around the fringes of the city, and one in Fiesole: Campeggio Panoramico (Camping Panorama) via Peramonda 1, Fiesole; Tel. (055) 599069. For details, contact the tourist office. Area Flog Pogetto, a service area for campers, with water and electric services, is located on via M. Mercati 24/b, Tel. (055) 481285. There is also a free emergency campsite with very limited facilities for stranded backpackers, the Area di Sosta, on the edge of town. It is open in summer only, and the location sometimes changes from year to year. Ask at the tourist information office for the address of the current site of a free emergency campsite for stranded backpackers (open in summer only).

May we camp here?   **Possiamo campeggiare qui?**

Is there a campsite near here? **C'è un campeggio qui vicino?**

We have a tent/caravan (trailer).   **Abbiamo la tenda/la roulotte.**

CAR RENTAL *(autonoleggio)* (See also DRIVING)
Although a car is not necessary for visiting Florence, Pisa, and Siena, having one gives you the freedom to explore Tuscany's out-of-the-way places inaccessible by public transport. There are numerous car rental firms in Florence. Rates vary considerably, and you should shop around for the lowest price.

The best rates are usually found by booking and paying for your car before you leave home, either directly through the office of an international rental company, or as part of a "fly-drive" package deal. Check that the quoted rate includes Collision Damage Waiver, unlimited mileage, and tax, as these can greatly increase the cost. Insurance costs are automatically covered by some credit cards; don't be double-charged.

Normally you must be over 21 to rent a car, and you will need to have held a full, valid driver's license (EU model for EU citizens) for at least 12 months (to be presented at time of rental). You will need to show your passport and produce a major credit card — cash deposits are prohibitively large. Almost all cars available are stick shifts; automatic rentals are limited in availability and far more costly.

I'd like to rent a car.   **Vorrei noleggiare una macchina.**

CLIMATE and CLOTHING
Summer is often oppressively hot and sticky (the hills surrounding Florence capture the heat and humidity), while midwinter can be unpleasantly cold. The wettest months are from October to April. The best times to visit are in spring and autumn, when temperatures are less extreme, but May and September have become extremely popular (and crowded) months to visit.

Florence

Approximate monthly average temperatures are as follows:

		J	F	M	A	M	J	J	A	S	O	N	D
°C	max	9	12	16	20	24	29	32	31	28	21	14	10
	min	2	2	5	5	12	15	17	17	15	11	6	3
°F	max	48	53	59	68	75	84	89	88	82	70	57	50
	min	35	36	40	46	53	59	62	61	59	52	43	37

Clothing. Cotton and linen clothes are best for coping with the summer heat, but you'll want a sweater or jacket on the cool evenings in spring and autumn. In winter, you will need warm clothes, a waterproof jacket, and an umbrella. Comfortable walking shoes for those cobbled streets are a must.

Remember that Florence's churches are places of worship as well as works of art and architecture, so dress respectably if you intend to visit them — shorts, miniskirts, and bare shoulders are frowned upon, and sometimes forbidden.

COMMUNICATIONS

E-mail *(posta elettronica)*. There are now several cyber-cafes and internet points located all over Florence. Internet Train has six locations in Florence, generally open daily 10am–11pm. They also offer scanning, printing, and fax services; Tel. (055) 214794. Some hotels offer e-mail access, too: Check with them before your arrive.

Post offices *(ufficio postale, PT)*. The central post office in Florence is on Via Pellicceria, just southwest of Piazza della Repubblica. It handles mail, telegrams, telex, fax services (to some but not all countries), and has a tourist information kiosk.

Open 8:15am–7pm Monday–Friday, 8:15am–noon Saturday; from 12:30pm–7pm Saturday afternoons, entry is accessible by a back door on piazza Davanzati (see also OPENING HOURS). Mail boxes are red — those marked *per la città* are for destinations within Florence, *per tutte le altre destinazioni* for all other destinations. The blue box is for express international post.

General delivery (*fermo posta*). If you're going to be in Florence without a secure address, you can receive "snail" mail at poste-restante (fermo posta) at the Via Pellicceria post office (see above). Don't forget your passport for identification when you go to pick up mail. Have mail addressed as follows:

> (Your Name)
> Fermo Posta
> Palazzo delle Poste
> 50100 Florence, Italy

Have you received any mail for…?	**C'è posta per…?**
I'd like a stamp for this letter/postcard.	**Desidero un francobollo per questa lettera/cartolina.**
airmail	**via aerea**
registered	**raccomandata**
I want to send a telegram to…	**Desidero mandare un telegramma a…**

Telephones (*telefono*). You can make local and international calls from the orange public telephones located all over the city, which accept coins. Many also accept phone cards (*scheda telefonica*), which can be bought from bar/tobacco stands (*tabacchi*) and news-stands and are available in €5 and €25. There is a convenient Telecom phone center located at Via Cavour, 21/r (open 7am–11pm), where you can purchase phone cards and find telephone books and usually a free and functioning phone.

To make an international call, dial 00, followed by the country code (**44** for UK, **1** for US), then the area code and number.

If you would like to use a calling card or make a collect call, the following are a list of access numbers for your country's toll free centers. (Note: You must always insert a coin or a card to access a line, even when making a toll-free call.)

US

AT&T 1721011	Sprint 1721877
MCI 1721022	Bell Atlantic 1721010
Bell South 1721025	

Canada

AT&T 1721002	Teleglobe 1721001

Australia

Optus 1721161	Telstra 1721061

New Zealand 1721064

Ireland 1720353

Malta 1720356

UK

BT 1720044	Automatic 1720144
Mercury 1720544	

To place collect calls or operator-assisted calls use the following numbers:

In Italy: **1795** International; **170** (English speaking operators)

For directory assistance:

In Italy: **12** International; **176** (English speaking operators)

Give me coins/a telephone card, please.	**Per favore, mi dia monette/ una scheda telefonica.**

CRIME

Florence is a fairly safe city, but you should take the usual precautions against theft — don't carry large amounts of cash, and leave your valuables in the hotel safe (not in your room, unless there is a room safe). Never leave your bags or valuables in view in a parked car; and never leave your bags in a car trunk overnight, even if out of sight. The only real danger is from possible pickpockets, especially in crowded areas, busy markets, and on public buses. If you have a shoulder bag, wear it across your body — it's harder to snatch.

Any theft or loss must be reported immediately to the police; obtain a copy of the report in order to comply with your travel insurance. If your passport is lost or stolen, inform your consulate immediately.

I want to report a theft.	**Voglio denunciare un furto.**
My wallet/passport/ticket has been stolen.	**Mi hanno rubato il portafoglio/il passaporto/ il biglietto.**

CUSTOMS *(dogana)* **and ENTRY FORMALITIES**
For citizens of EU countries, a valid passport or identity card is needed to enter Italy for stays of up to 90 days. Citizens of Australia, New Zealand, and the US also require only a valid passport.

Visas *(permesso di soggiorno).* For stays of more than 90 days a special visa or residence permit is required. Visa regulations change from time to time; for full information on passport and visa regulations check with the Italian Embassy in your country.

Free exchange of non-duty-free goods for personal use is allowed between EU countries. For residents of non-EU countries, restrictions when returning home are as follows:

Into:	cigarettes	cigars		tobacco	alcohol	wine		beer
Australia:	250		250 or	250g	1*l*			
Canada:	200	and 50	and	400*g*	1.14*l* or	1.1*l* or	8.5*l*	
New Zealand:	200	or 50	or	250g	1*l*	and 4.5*l* or	4.5*l*	
South Africa:	400	and 50	and	250g	1*l*	and	2*l*	
USA:	200	or 50	or	2*kg*	1*l*	or	1*l*	

Florence

Currency restrictions. Tourists may bring an unlimited amount of Italian or foreign currency into the country. On departure you must declare any currency beyond the equivalent of €10,300, so it's wise to declare sums exceeding this amount when you arrive.

DRIVING in ITALY

Motorists planning to take their vehicle into Italy need a full driver's license, an International Motor Insurance Certificate, and a Vehicle Registration Document. A green insurance card is not a legal requirement, but it is strongly recommended for travel within Italy. Foreign visitors must display an official nationality sticker, and, if coming from the U.K. or Ireland, headlights must be adjusted for driving on the right. Full details are available from your automobile association, insurance company, or embassy.

The use of seatbelts is obligatory; fines for non-compliance are stiff. A red warning triangle must be carried in case of breakdown. Motorcycle riders must wear helmets.

Driving conditions. Drive on the right, pass on the left. Give way to traffic coming from the right. Speed limits: 50 km/h (30 mph) in town, 90 km/h (55 mph) on freeways, and 130 km/h (80 mph) on highways.

The freeways (*superstrada*) and most highways (*autostrada*) are excellent. Florence lies near the famed Autostrada del Sole (A1), which runs the length of Italy, allowing fast road connections with Bologna, Milan, Rome, and Naples. Italian autostradas (indicated by green signs) are toll roads — you take an entry ticket from an automatic machine when you enter the highway, and pay at the other end for the distance traveled.

Traffic police *(polizia stradale).* Italian traffic police are authorized to impose on-the-spot fines for speeding and other traffic offenses, such as driving while intoxicated or stopping in a no-stopping zone. All cities, and many towns and villages, have signs posted at the outskirts indicating the telephone number of the local traffic police headquarters or Carabinieri (see POLICE). Police have recently become stricter about speeding.

Should you be involved in a road accident, dial **112** for the Carabinieri. If your car is stolen or broken into, contact the Urban Police Headquarters (Questura) in Florence at Via Zara 2, and get a copy of their report for your insurance claim.

Gasoline *(benzina)* Gasoline (petrol) is sold in three, soon to be only two, grades. The grades available are Super (98–100 octane), Normal (86–88 octane), and Senza Piombo (unleaded — look for the pumps with green labels marked senza piombo or SP). Be aware that a station marked "Gas" indicates that it has methane gas and may not offer unleaded gasoline in addition.

Driving in Florence. The center of Florence (within the circle of avenues or *viali* that surrounds it on both sides of the River Arno) is a restricted ZTL area (*zona traffico limitato* — limited traffic zone): Between 7:30am and 6:30pm Monday–Saturday, only residents with special permits on their windshields are allowed into this zone. Traffic police are usually stationed at the major entry roads to stop anyone without a permit. Tourists may enter to offload baggage and passengers at their hotel (carrying a faxed confirmation from your hotel to facilitate entry); you must then go and park outside the ZTL. If you can speak Italian, ask a policeman for directions, as the one-way system is rather complex.

Parking *(parcheggio).* Even if you make it into the city center after 6:30pm, or on a Sunday, it is virtually impossible to park on the street, but you can pay to park in one of the 70-plus official lots. Parking in the street is generally reserved for residents 8am–8pm. Apart from the city-center parking places, there are others at Porta Romana (left bank), the Cascine (Piazza Vittorio Veneto), and

Florence

Fortezza da Basso (Viale Filippo Strozzi). A smaller — but convenient — car park is located in Piazza Libertà. There is a very new system for parking on some streets indicated by blue painted markers. From 8am–8pm you can pre-pay an estimated time using an often semi-hidden meter marked with a white "P" on a blue background; place the issued ticket inside your windshield.

If you park your car on the street overnight in the center of Florence, be extremely careful to heed the restrictions posted on parking signs. Fines are very heavy and the city is well-equipped to remove illegally parked cars and tow them to the car pound (via Olmatelo in the periphery called Novoli). If this should happen, call (or ask your hotel to call) the municipal police, Tel. (055) 308249 to locate your car. You'll need to go there in person with documents and pay a stiff fine to get it back. It is every visitor's nightmare.

Breakdown. In the event of a breakdown, find a telephone and dial **116**. This will put you in touch with the ACI (Automobile Club d'Italia), the national automobile organization. About every 2 km (1½ miles or so) on the autostrada there's an emergency call box marked "SOS."

Road signs. Most road signs in Italy are international. Here are some written signs you might also come across:

Curva pericolosa	Dangerous bend/curve
Deviazione	Detour
Divieto di sorpasso	No passing
Divieto di sosta	No stopping
Lavori in corso	Road works/Men working
Pericolo	Danger
Rallentare	Slow down
Senso vietato/unico	No entry/One-way street

Vietato l'ingresso	No entry
Zona pedonale	Pedestrian zone
ZTL	Limited traffic zone
(International) Driving License	**patente (internazionale)**
car registration papers	**libretto di circolazione**
Green Card	**carta verde**
Can I park here?	**Posso parcheggiare qui?**
Are we on the right road for…?	**Siamo sulla strada giusta per…?**
Fill the tank please…	**Per favore, faccia il pieno di…**
super/normal	**super/normale**
lead-free/diesel	**senza piombo/gasolio**
I've had a breakdown.	**Ho avuto un guasto.**
There's been an accident.	**C'è stato un incidente.**

E

ELECTRIC CURRENT
220V/50Hz AC is standard. An adapter for continental-style sockets will be needed; American 110V appliances also require a transformer.

an adapter	**una presa complementare**

EMBASSIES and CONSULATES
In Florence:

UK (consulate): Lungarno Corsini, 2; Tel. (055) 284133

US (consulate): Lungarno A. Vespucci, 38; Tel. (055) 2398276/217605

Florence

South Africa (consulate): Piazza Salterelli, 1; Tel. (055) 281863

In Rome:
Australia (HC): Via Alessandria, 215; Tel.(06) 852721

Canada (HC): Via Zara, 30; Tel.(06)445981

New Zealand (embassy): Via Zara, 28; Tel.(06)4417171

Republic of Ireland (embassy): Via G. Medici, 1; Tel. (06)5810777

EMERGENCIES

If you don't speak Italian, find a local resident to help you, or talk to the English-speaking operator on the telephone assisted service, Tel. **170**.

Police	**112**
General Emergency	**113**
Fire	**115**
Paramedics	**118**

Please, can you place an emergency call to the…?	**Per favore, può fare una telefonata d'emergenza…?**
police	**alla polizia**
fire brigade	**ai pompieri**
hospital	**all'ospedale**

ETIQUETTE

Italians appreciate good manners. When you enter a shop, restaurant, or office, the greeting is always *buon giorno* (good morning) or *buona sera* (good afternoon/evening — used from around 1pm onwards). When inquiring, start with *per favore* (please), and for any service rendered say *grazie* (thanks), to which the reply is *prego* (don't mention it, you're welcome). Accompany a handshake with *piacere* (it's a pleasure). A more familiar greeting, used among friends and popular with younger people, is *ciao* (pronounced "chow"), which means both "Hi" and "see you later." In churches, shorts, miniskirts, or bare shoulders are not considered respectable.

G

GAY and LESBIAN TRAVELERS
Florence historically has been tolerant of gays. There are several gay bar/discos; a good reference is a magazine called *Spartacus International Gay Guide,* available at the newsstand in Piazza Santa Maria Novella. You may also want to contact ARCI-gay, the national gay rights organization, whose local office is Via S. Zanobi, 54/r; Tel. (055) 476557 (office hours); or Lesbian Line, for advice and information; Tel. (055) 488288 (open 4pm–8pm Monday–Friday).

GUIDES and TOURS *(guide, gite)*
Most major hotels can arrange or provide multilingual guides or interpreters for one-on-one or small groups. Alternatively you can hire one independently through the Tuscan Tourist Guides Society:

> **AGT Ass.,** Via Calimala, 2; Tel./fax (055) 2645217;
> e-mail <agt@arca.net>.

A number of organized two- and three-hour walking tours of the historical center are less expensive and are an enjoyable and educational way to orient yourself: Hotels and tourist offices will have details.

A number of travel agencies and bus companies offer organized bus tours of the countryside around Florence, including excursions to San Gimignano/Siena or Pisa. Details can be obtained through your hotel, the tourist information office, and local travel agencies.

We'd like an English-speaking guide.	**Desideriamo una guida che parla inglese.**
I need an English interpreter.	**Ho bisogno di un interprete d'inglese.**

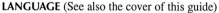

L

LANGUAGE (See also the cover of this guide)
English is generally spoken in Florence (especially by the young people), and you can get by without a word of Italian, but it is polite to learn at least a few basic phrases. Local people will welcome and encourage any attempt you make to use their language.

LAUNDRY and DRY-CLEANING *(lavanderia, tintoria)*
Launderettes and dry-cleaners are worth seeking out because hotels can charge high prices and often require a few days. There are several self-service launderettes in Florence called **Wash & Dry** where you can do small loads of washing at much better rates. They are open daily 8am–9pm and are located on Via dei Servi, 105/r; Via Nazionale, 129/r; and via dei Serragli, 87/r. There is also Onda Blu on via degli Alfani, 24/r open everyday from 8am-10pm; toll free tel. 800 861 346. For a dry-cleaners (tintoria) ask your hotel for the closest location.

When will it be ready?	**Quando sarà pronto?**
I must have this for tomorrow morning.	**Mi serve per domani mattina.**

LOST PROPERTY *(oggetti smarriti)*
Ask for advice from your hotel or the local tourist information office before contacting the police. For items left behind on public transport, ask your hotel to telephone the bus or train station or taxi company. Lost property that has been handed in to the police has to be claimed at the City Council Lost Property Office *(Ufficio dei Oggetti Smarriti del Comune)*, Via Circondaria, 19; Tel. (055) 3283942.

I've lost my passport/wallet/bag/purse.	**Ho perso il passaporto/il portafoglio/la borsa/la borsetta.**

MEDIA

Newspapers and magazines *(giornali; riviste)*. The Florence-based national newspaper, *La Nazione*, provides national and international news, features, and useful restaurant reviews and entertainment listings. *La Repubblica* also has a Florence edition. You can find newspapers in English in city-center newsstands. *The International Herald Tribune* is available on the day of publication. A free booklet called *Concierge Information* is available from most hotels and contains a lot of handy information, including museum hours, special museum exhibits, train and bus timetables, and useful addresses.

Radio and TV *(radio, televisione)*. Italy's state-sponsored TV network, the RAI *(Radio televisione italiana)*, broadcasts three TV channels, which compete with six independent channels. All programs are in Italian, including British and American feature films and imports, which are dubbed. CNN (in English) is transmitted on channel 7 in the morning from 6–8am (hotels with cable offer 24-hour CNN coverage). The airwaves are crammed with Italian-language radio stations, most of them broadcasting popular music. The BBC World Service can be picked up on 648KHz AM.

MEDICAL CARE (see also EMERGENCIES)

EU citizens are entitled to free emergency hospital treatment if they have form E111 (obtainable from a post office before leaving home). You may have to pay part of the price of treatment or medicine; if so, remember to keep receipts so that you can claim a refund when you return home. The special social clinic (ASL) for foreigners is *Assistenza Medica A Stranieri In Italia*, Borgognissanti, 20; Tel. (055) 2285501 (open Monday–Saturday 8am–noon and Wednesdays also from 2:30–4:30pm).

Florence

If you should need the services of an interpreter in a medical situation, contact the Associazione Volontari Ospedalieri, a group of volunteer interpreters who are always on call, and offer their telephone services free; Tel. (055) 2344567.

The American Consulate recommends the English-speaking walk-in clinic of Giorgio Scappini, Via Bonifaciolupi, 32; Tel. (055) 483363 or (0330) 774731.

It is recommended to obtain travel insurance before you leave home to be sure you are covered; ask your travel agent for details.

Most pharmacies (*farmacie*) follow retail hours; the one in the Santa Maria Novella railway station stays open all night. On weekends or public holidays, the addresses of pharmacists on duty are published in the newspaper *La Nazione* and are also posted on every farmacia door. In Italy, pharmacists are able to diagnose and prescribe mild medication for which, elsewhere, you would normally need a prescription. If it is not a true emergency, make a visit to a pharmacist instead of the hospital. No vaccinations are required for entry into Italy.

I need a doctor/a dentist.	**Ho bisogno di un medico/ dentista.**
It hurts here.	**Ho un dolore qui.**
a stomach ache	**un mal di stomaco**
a fever	**la febbre**
sunburn/sunstroke	**una scottatura di sole/un colpo di sole**

MONEY MATTERS
Currency. In common with most other European countries, the official currency used in Italy is the euro (€). Notes are in denominations of 5, 10, 20, 50, 100 and 500 euros; coins in 1 and 2 euros and 1, 2, 5, 10, 20 and 50 cents.

Banks and currency exchange offices. Banking hours are generally 8:30am–1pm and 3–4pm Monday–Friday. The exchange offices on Via dei Calzaiuoli, between the Duomo and Piazza della Signoria, are open all day and on weekends. There is also an exchange counter (*cambio*) in the railway station, open 8:20am–7:20pm Monday–Saturday. Commission charges can be high, around €2–3 per transaction or according to the amount exchanged; it is almost always posted, often in small print. Taking cash advances from an ATM (*bancomat*) usually offers the best exchange rate: Check with your bank at home to make sure that your account is authorized for international withdrawals and that your PIN-number is the appropriate number of digits. Look for correlating symbols on the cash machine and the back of your card. American Express has a full-service office for their clients on via Dante Alighieri 22r, near the Duomo.

Travelers checks and credit cards. In the main tourist areas, almost everyone accepts travelers checks, though you're likely to get a better exchange rate at a bank. You'll usually need your passport to cash a travelers check. Keep your remaining checks in the hotel safe, if possible. At the very least, be sure to keep your receipt and a list of the serial numbers of the checks in a separate place to facilitate a refund in case of loss or theft. All major credit cards are usually accepted by hotels, restaurants, car-rental firms, and other businesses; look for the symbols on the door to be sure. Visa is more widely accepted than American Express.

Planning Your Budget

To give you an idea of what to expect, here's a list of typical (but approximate) prices:.

Car rental. Check with your local rental agency for up-to-the - minute deals and book before you leave. One-day rental rates are extremely high; weekly rates better. Be sure to ask if rates include taxes, unlimited mileage, and insurance coverage.

Entertainment: Cinema €7, club (entry and first drink) €15–25, outdoor opera €15–50.

Hotels: (double room with bath, including tax and service, high-season rates): 5-star from €450, 4-star over €225–450, 3-star €150–225, 2-star €100–150, 1-star under €100.

Meals and drinks: Continental breakfast €8, lunch/dinner in fairly good establishment €18–30, coffee served at a table €2–3.50, served at the bar €0.50–1. Also at the bar: bottle of beer €1.50–2, soft drinks €1.50–3, aperitif €3 and up.

Museums Admission fees range from around €2 for the small, church museums to between €6.50 and €10 for the major collections. See also pages 78–80.

I want to change some pounds/ dollars/travelers checks.	**Desidero cambiare delle sterline/dei dollari/ "traveler's checks"**
Can I pay with this credit card?	**Posso pagare con la carta di credito?**
Where is the bank/ATM?	**Dov'è il banco/bancomat?**

OPENING HOURS

Banks. 8:30am–1pm, and 3–4pm Monday–Friday.

Museums and art galleries. See pages 78–80.

Post offices. 8:15am–7pm Monday–Friday, 8:15am–noon and 12:30pm–7pm Saturday (accessible by a back door on piazza Davanzati, Saturday afternoons).

Shops. Although many of the large stores and supermarkets now remain open all day (*no-stop* or *orario continuato*), the majority still adhere to the decades-old Florentine tradition of closing for a long lunch and on Monday mornings (Wednesday afternoons for food shops). Generally, shop opening hours are: Mondays 3:30–7.30pm and Tuesday to Saturday 8:30 or 9:00am–1pm and 3:30 or 4–7 or 8pm. Food shops tend to open earlier than this and close earlier, while clothes shops may do the opposite, often not opening until 10am. Some of the central Florentine stores remain open for some part of Sunday but many still close on that day. There are a limited number of stores open during the month of August, and if you see a sign that says *chiuso per ferie* with dates, it indicates they are closed for vacation and usually indicates the date when they will reopen. Good shopping times in Italy are the two legal sales periods (*saldi*): from the second week of January to the second week of February, and mid-August to mid-September.

 P

PHOTOGRAPHY and VIDEO (*fotografia, video*)
Major brands of film and video cassettes are widely available, but they are expensive, so stock up before you leave. Photo shops in Florence can process your color prints in 24–48 hours at reasonable prices, and some provide a 1-hour service. Be aware when buying blank or pre-recorded video cassettes that Italy uses the European PAL system, not the American NECJ.

Be aware that the use of flash or tripod is forbidden in most museums and cathedrals.

I'd like a film for this camera.	**Vorrei una pellicola per questa macchina.**
a color-slide film	**una pellicola di diapositive**
a film for color prints	**una pellicola per fotografie a colori**

How long will it take to develop this film?	**Quanto tempo ci vuole per sviluppare questa pellicola?**
May I take a picture?	**Posso fare una fotografia?**

POLICE *(polizia)*

Florence's city police, the Vigili Urbani, handle traffic and parking and perform other routine tasks. While the officers rarely speak English, they are courteous and helpful towards tourists. The Carabinieri, a paramilitary force, wear light brown or blue uniforms with peaked caps, and deal with more serious crimes and demonstrations. Outside town, the Polizia Stradale patrol the highways, issue speeding tickets, and assist with breakdowns (see also DRIVING).

Vigili Urbani Headquarters (Questura) and Stolen Vehicles Department; Tel. (055) 49771

Carabinieri Regional Headquarters (the only station where you're more likely to find someone who speaks English): Borgo Ognissanti, 48; Tel. (055)24811

Polizia Stradale (Traffic Police); Tel. (055) 577777

Where's the nearest police station?	**Dov'è il più vicino punto di polizia?**

PUBLIC HOLIDAYS *(feste)*

Banks, offices, government institutions, most shops, and many museums are closed on national holidays, as well as on the Florentines' local holiday on 24 June, commemorating the town's patron saint, San Giovanni Battista (St. John the Baptist). During the long weekend of 15 August, almost everything in Florence (and Italy) closes, except hotels, a few shops, pharmacies, cafés, restaurants, and some of the major tourist attractions. Most make a week (or longer) of it.

1 January	*Capodanno or Primo dell'Anno*	New Year's Day
6 January	*Epifania*	Epiphany

25 April	*Festa della Liberazione*	Liberation Day
1 May	*Festa del Lavoro*	Labor Day
24 June	*San Giovanni*	Patron Saint of Florence
15 August	*Ferragosto*	Feast of the Assumption
1 November	*Ognissanti*	All Saints' Day
8 December	*Concezione Immacolata*	Immaculate Conception
25 December	*Natale*	Christmas Day
26 December	*Santo Stefano*	St. Stephen's Day

Movable dates:

Pasqua	Easter
Lunedi di Pasqua	Easter Monday

 R

RELIGION *(religione)*
Italy is an overwhelmingly Roman Catholic country, with Catholicism accounting for 83% of the population. Mass is celebrated in English in the Duomo every Saturday at 5pm, and in the Church of San Giovanni di Dio, Borgognissanti, 16–20, on Sundays and holidays at 10am. Many other denominations are represented in Florence; for details, contact the tourist information office (see TOURIST INFORMATION OFFICES).

T

TIME DIFFERENCES
Italian time coincides with most of Western Europe — Greenwich Mean Time plus one hour. In summer, an hour is added for Daylight Saving Time.

New York	London	**Florence**	Sydney	Auckland
6am	11am	**noon**	8pm	10pm

Florence

What time is it? **Che ore sono?**

TIPPING *(la mancia)*

Though a service charge is commonly added to most restaurant bills (look for *servizio incluso*), it is customary to leave a small additional tip. If service charge is not included, 10–15% is the norm. It is also in order to tip bellboys, doormen, and lavatory attendants for their service. Taxi drivers do not expect a full 10% (except from foreigner passengers), and normal practice by Italians is simply to round up the fare.

TOILETS *(gabinetti)*

You will find public toilets in airports, railway and bus stations, museums, and art galleries; they are often designated by the sign "WC." The men's may be indicated by "U" (uomini), or "signori," the ladies' by "D" (donne), or "signore." Don't confuse signori and signore!

Where are the toilets? **Dove sono i gabinetti?**

TOURIST INFORMATION OFFICES

The Italian State Tourist Office, or ENIT (Ente Nazionale Italiano per il Turismo), maintains offices in many countries throughout the world. A few are listed below:

Canada: 1 Place Ville-Marie, Suite 1914, Montreal H3B 3M9, Quebec; Tel. (514) 866-7667

Ireland: 47 Merrion Square, Dublin 2; Tel. (01) 766397

UK: 1 Princes Street, London W1R 8AY; Tel. (020) 7408-1254

US: 401 N. Michigan Avenue, Chicago, IL 60611; Tel. (312) 644-0990. 630 Fifth Avenue, New York, NY 10111; Tel. (212) 245-4822.

In Italy, the provincial tourist information offices are the APT (Azienda di Promozione Turistica), <www.firenze.turismo.

toscana.it>, <apt@firenze.turismo.toscana.it>. They have English-speaking staff, and can provide free maps and general advice and information. The APT offices in Florence and nearby are listed below:

Florence: Via A. Manzoni, 16; Tel. (055) 523320, fax (055) 2346286 (8am–7pm Monday–Saturday. The following are more central: Via Cavour, 1r; Tel. (055) 290832 (8am–7pm Monday–Saturday)

Borgo S. Croce, 29/r; Tel. (055) 2340444 (8am–7pm daily in summer, 9am–3pm Monday–Saturday in winter)

Piazza Stazione, 4; Tel. (055) 212245 (8am–7pm Monday–Saturday)

A Jubilee 2000 information office hopes to stay open after the Jubilee ends: Piazza Duomo 57/r; Tel. (055) 291239, fax (055) 2645240 (daily 9am–6pm); <infogiubileofi@mclink.it>

Fiesole: Via Portigiani, 3; Tel. (055) 598720 (10am–6pm Monday–Saturday)

Siena: Via di Città 43; Tel. (0577) 42209; (8:30am–7:30pm Monday–Saturday) and Piazza del Campo 56; Tel. (0577) 280551 (daily 8:30am–7:30pm)

Pisa: Via Cammeo, 2; Tel. (050) 560464; (9:30am–noon, 3–5:30pm, closed Sunday afternoon and Monday morning).

TRANSPORT
Buses. The orange ATAF buses provide a cheap and efficient way of getting around the city and its suburbs (although in the pedestrian-only center, almost everything is within walking distance). Before you board, buy your ticket from shops and news-stands displaying an orange Biglietti Abbonamenti Ataf Qui ("bus passes here"); stamp it in the yellow box on the bus (Ataf officials periodically conduct spot checks to make sure tickets have been

stamped; they impose stiff fines on ticket-holders who have not stamped their tickets, no excuses accepted). Tickets are valid for one, two, or 24 hours, and you can make as many journeys as you like, as long as they begin within the period of validity (you only punch the ticket once, on the first bus you use). Tourists can also buy a Carta Arancio (Orange Card), which gives seven days' unlimited travel on buses and trains within the province of Florence (this does not include Pisa or Siena, just Florence and its suburbs). For details of timetables and routes, ask at the ATAF information office outside the railway station or at Piazza del Duomo 57/r.

A number of other bus companies provide inter-city services to destinations further afield, including Siena, Perugia, Rome, and Milan. The main companies include SITA, Tel. (055) 47821 or (800) 373760, whose station and information office is on Viale dei Cadorna, 105, and Lazzi, Tel. (055) 215154, in Piazza Stazione; they are on opposites sides of the main railway station.

Taxis. Taxis can be picked up at ranks in the main city squares, or called by telephone (Tel. (055) 4499 or (055) 4242) but not hailed. Fares are recorded on the meter, and there are extra charges for luggage, radio calls, Sunday and late-night trips. It is normal practice to round up the fare.

Trains. The Italian State Railway, FS (Ferrovie dello Stato), has an excellent rail network. Florence's Santa Maria Novella station is well-designed and efficient, with regular services to Rome, Milan, Venice (to name but a few), and other European cities. In addition to the information office, there are a number of computerized information points, where you can get train times and fares from a touch-screen terminal. Large postings of *arrivi* (arrivals) and *partenze* (departures) are especially helpful. Prices are reasonable, particularly those for second-class travel. To pay with a credit card, look for the credit card sticker in the window to make sure you're standing in the right line. Some ticket machines take credit cards as well as cash. Be aware of the infamous Italian *sciopero* or train strikes (less frequent these days than in the past) that can last from a few hours to a few days. Try to check with your hotel before going to the station, as strikes are always announced and publicized in the paper and on the news the day before, if not sooner.

When's the next bus/ train to …?	**Quando parte il prossimo autobus/treno per…?**
single (one-way)/	**andata/**
return (round-trip)	**andata e ritorno**
first/second class	**prima/seconda classe**
What's the fare to…?	**Qual è la tariffa per…?**

TRAVELERS with DISABILITIES

Florence is not an easy city for disabled travelers. Many of the more popular attractions are equipped with ramps for wheelchair access, but public transport is a problem, as are hotels, restaurants, and most minor attractions. Contact a tourist information office for details about accessible hotels, galleries, and museums, and for addresses of Italian associations for the disabled.

TRAVELING to FLORENCE

By Air

The best deal on scheduled flights is the advanced-purchase fare of a weekday departure, which must be booked at least seven or 14 days in advance, and include a Saturday night abroad.

From the UK and US, there are scheduled flights from the major cities to the international gateway airports of Rome and Milan, where you can catch a connecting flight to Pisa or Florence. Nonstop flights from the UK connect London with Pisa (and occasionally Florence); direct flights to and from New

Florence

York/Pisa do not yet exist. Charter flights and package deals are available from both the US and the UK — check with your travel agent for the latest deals.

On-line booking is a popular way to cash in on some great air-fare deals. Among the growing numbers of reliable, money-saving on-line sites, register with Travelocity (<www.travelocity.com>) to have the lowest fares sent directly to your e-mail address. Preview Travel's site (<www.reservations.com>) will quote you the three best fares according to your personalized specifications.

Charter flights and package tours. Rail-package deals departing from London's Victoria Station are also available. Florence is also featured in all-inclusive packages that include Rome, Tuscany, or the Italian Lakes.

It is also possible to get a seat on a charter flight on a flight-only basis, generally cheaper than a high-season ticket on a scheduled flight. However, charters are less flexible, with perhaps only two flights weekly, and there are restrictions attached which should be checked out at the start. Cancellation insurance is recommended.

By Road

A coach service runs from London Victoria to Florence. For drivers taking their own vehicles, the fastest route from the UK is via Paris and the A6 Autoroute du Soleil to near Macon, then east on the A40 and through the Mont Blanc Tunnel to Turin, Genoa, and finally Florence.

The most direct rail route from Britain is the daily boat train from London Victoria to Paris (or the faster Eurostar "Chunnel" train to Paris), where you change to the overnight sleeper train to Florence; the full voyage takes approximately 22 hours, and the ticket is only slightly cheaper than travelling by air. If you are touring Europe by rail, the following passes can be used in Italy: Inter-

Rail, Rail Europ Senior, Eurailpass, Eurail Youthpass, and other Eurail passes.

Italian State Railways offer fare reductions in certain cases. The BTLC Tourist Ticket (Biglietto Turistico di Libera Circolozione) is valid for specified periods of unlimited travel within Italy in first or second class, and the Kilometric Ticket (Biglietto Chilometrico) can be used by up to 5 people for up to 20 journeys totaling a maximum of 3,000 person-km (i.e., 1,500 km each for two people, 600 km each for five). These tickets can be purchased at home or in Italy.

 W

WATER *(acqua)*
There are numerous old drinking fountains in Florence's parks and piazzas. Tap water is safe *(potabile)*, but mineral water is more palatable.

a bottle of mineral water	**una bottiglia di acqua minerale**
still/fizzy	**naturale/frizzante gasata**

WEIGHTS and MEASURES
Fluid measures

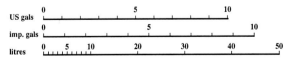

Distance

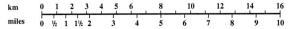

Florence

Length

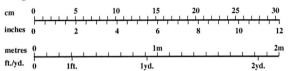

| cm | 0 | | 5 | | 10 | | 15 | | 20 | | 25 | | 30 |
| inches | 0 | | 2 | | 4 | | 6 | | 8 | | 10 | | 12 |

| metres | 0 | | | 1m | | | 2m |
| ft./yd. | 0 | | 1ft. | | 1yd. | | 2yd. |

Weight

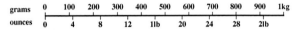

| grams | 0 | 100 | 200 | 300 | 400 | 500 | 600 | 700 | 800 | 900 | 1kg |
| ounces | 0 | 4 | 8 | 12 | 1lb | 20 | 24 | 28 | 2lb |

Temperature

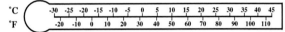

| °C | -30 | -25 | -20 | -15 | -10 | -5 | 0 | 5 | 10 | 15 | 20 | 25 | 30 | 35 | 40 | 45 |
| °F | -20 | -10 | 0 | 10 | 20 | 30 | 40 | 50 | 60 | 70 | 80 | 90 | 100 | 110 |

Y

YOUTH HOSTELS *(ostelli della gioventù)*

Contact your national youth hostel association before departure to obtain an international membership card. Of the three hostels in Florence, the most central is in the historic center of town on the Left Bank between Santo Spirito and Piazza del Carmine — the Ostello Santa Monaca, Via Santa Monaca, 6; Tel. (055) 268338; <www.ostello.it; info@ostello.it>. There is also a popular hostel complete with swimming pool called "Youth Firenze 2000" that is open summer months only: Viale R. Sanzio, 16; Tel. (055) 2335558; fax (055) 2306392; <european@dada.it>. The Italian Youth Hostel Association (Associazione Italiana Alberghi per la Gioventù) has one hostel in a converted villa on the outskirts of Florence, a 30-minute bus trip from the center in Fiesole: Ostello Europa Villa Camerata, Viale A. Righi, 4; Tel. (055) 601451; fax (055) 610300. In the Tuscan countryside 30 km (19 miles) from Florence is the Ostello del Chianti, Via Roma, 137 Tavernelle Val di Pesa; Tel. (055) 8077009.

Recommended Hotels

During the high season from April–November (the nice-weather months of May/June and September are most popular), accommodation in Florence is at a premium, and you should try to book a room as far in advance as possible. In fact, reservations are always strongly recommended, especially for the smaller, lower-priced hotels (with lots of conventions and trade fairs, Florence can fill up even when not expected in off months). However, if you do arrive in Florence without a reservation, the ITA office at Santa Maria Novella railway station will find a room for you (see Handy Travel Tips: Accommodation, page 100).

As a basic guide, we have used the symbols below to indicate published rack rates per night for a standard double room with bath, including all taxes, service, and breakfast. Some hotels discount during the low season, so it is always worth trying to bargain.

€€€€	over €225
€€€	€150–225
€€	€100–150
€	under €100

Annalena €€€ *Via Romana, 34, 50125 Florence; Tel. (055) 222402; fax 222403; <www.hotelannalena.it>*. Tasteful hotel on first floor of a historically important palazzo from the 14th century; many rooms share a terrace overlooking a lovely private garden. Located across from the Pitti Palace and Boboli Gardens. 20 rooms. Major credit cards.

Astoria Pullman €€€€ *Via del Giglio 9, 50123 Florence; Tel. (055) 239 8095; fax 214632; <astoria.boscolohotels.com>*. Fine old Florentine palazzo, part of which dates from the 13th and 14th centuries, offering gracious rooms. Centrally located equidistant to the Duomo and open-air market of San Lorenzo. 102 rooms. Major credit cards.

Baglioni €€€€ *Piazza Unità Italiana, 6, 50123 Florence; Tel. (055) 23580; fax 2358895; <www.hotelbaglioni.it>*. A dignified, well-run hotel just across the square from the railway station. A turn-of-the-century bastion that boasts a roof-terrace restaurant offering fantastic views. 195 rooms. Major credit cards.

Balestri €€–€€€ *Piazza Mentana, 7 (Lungarno Diaz), 50122 Florence; Tel. (055) 214743; fax 2398042; <www.hotel-balestri.it>*. Family-run hotel established in the 19th century, on river bank, within striking distance of the Uffizi. No frills, but homey, comfortable, and a longtime favorite. 46 rooms. Major credit cards.

Beacci Tornabuoni €€€ *Via dei Tornabuoni, 3, 50123 Florence; Tel. (055) 212645; fax 283594; <www.BThotel.it>*. Classic Florentine *pensione*-like hotel on high floor of a 14th-century palazzo on the city's premier designer-lined shopping street. Old-fashioned elegance with a homey atmosphere and new owners. 29 rooms. Major credit cards.

Bellettini € *Via dei Conti, 7, 50123 Florence; Tel. (055) 213561; fax 283551; <www.firenze.net/hotelbellettini>*. Pleasant hotel with cheerfully, carefully decorated rooms, near the San Lorenzo street market. Use of internet and impressively abundant breakfast included in room rate. 27 rooms. Major credit cards.

Bernini Palace €€€€ *Piazza San Firenze 29, 50122 Florence; Tel. (055) 288621; fax 268272; <www.baglionihotels.com>*. Atmospheric hotel in a centuries-old palazzo at the back of the Palazzo Vecchio, popular with business men for its excellent location and fine service. 85 rooms. Major credit cards.

Brunelleschi €€€€ *Piazza Santa Elizabetta 3, 50122 Florence;
Tel. (055) 27370; fax 219653;* *<www.hotelbrunelleschi.it>*. Built
on Roman foundations, this hotel has its own small medieval
museum, and incorporates the adjoining Torre della Pagliazza
into the premises — all on its own tiny little piazza in the shadow of the Duomo. 96 rooms. Major credit cards.

Casci € *Via Cavour, 13, 50129 Florence; Tel. (055) 211686; fax
2396461;* *<www.hotelcasci.com>*. Simple, tastefully renovated
rooms in a 15th-century building that was once the home of G.
Rossini, the composer of *Barber of Seville*. Run by an amiable
family, and an easy stroll from the Duomo. 25 rooms. Major
credit cards.

Cimabue €€ *Via Benifacio Lupi, 7, 50129 Florence; Tel. (055)
471989; fax 475601.* Set in a quiet residential section just outside
the center, a charming setting with hospitable hosts. A leisurely
half-hour stroll to the Duomo. 16 rooms. Major credit cards.

Excelsior €€€€ *Piazza Ognissanti, 3, 50123 Florence; Tel.
(055) 264201; fax 210278;* *<www.luxurycollection.com/excel-
siorflorence>*. Old-fashioned elegance in Florence's grande dame
hotel, on the banks of the Arno. Recently refurbished with plush
carpets, chaise-lounges, and spacious bathrooms in the guest
rooms and grand public rooms. 168 rooms. Major credit cards.

Firenze € *Piazza Donati, 4, 50122 Florence; Tel. (055)
268301; fax 212370.* This very central bargain is ideal for the
traveler looking for an unfussy atmosphere and equipped, nice-
ly tiled bathrooms. Rooms (all with bathrooms) are simple, but
a good value for your lire. 61 rooms. No credit cards.

Grand €€€€ *Piazza Ognissanti, 1, 50123 Florence; Tel. (055)
288781; fax 217400;* *<www.luxurycollection.com/grandeflo-*

Florence

rence>. Sister hotel to (and located across the piazza from) the Excelsior — both are run by the Starwood group. Similar level of luxury, but with a slightly more intimate and less commercialized ambience, some rooms with Renaissance-style frescoes. Recently refurbished. 107 rooms. Major credit cards.

Il Guelfo Bianco €€€ *Via Cavour, 29, 50129 Florence; Tel. (055) 288330; fax 295203; <www.ilguelfobianco.it>.* An early 1990s newcomer in a 15th-century palazzo, furnished with some original antiques and with a friendly but correct staff, just north of the Duomo. 39 rooms. Major credit cards.

Hermitage €€€ *Vicolino Marzio, 1, 50122 Florence; Tel. (055) 287216; fax 212208; <www.italyhotel.com/firenze/hermitage>.* Romantic and central — reach out and touch the Ponte Vecchio. Housed in a 13th-century tower and invitingly decorated with oriental runners and potted palms. A top-floor alfresco breakfast terrace offers sweeping views enjoyed by some of the newly refurbished rooms as well. 28 rooms. Major credit cards.

Lungarno €€€€ *Borgo S. Jacopo, 14, 50125 Florence; Tel. (055) 27261; fax 268437; <www.lungarnohotels.com>.* The only hotel directly on the (south) banks of the Arno, with half of its newly renovated rooms overlooking the Ponte Vecchio. Owned by the local scions of style and fashion, the Ferragamo family. Some rooms housed in an adjacent 15th-century tower. 69 rooms. Major credit cards.

Kraft €€€€ *Via Solferino, 2, 50123 Florence; Tel. (055) 284273; fax 239 8267; e-mail <hotel.kraft@ firenzealbergo. it>.* Friendly hotel just a block from the Arno whose return guests are theater-goers and performers at the nearby Teatro Comunale, Florence's opera house. Many rooms overlook the river. Small but enjoyable roof-top swimming pool — a rarity in town. Not the most conveneint location of those listed here. 80 rooms. Major credit cards.

Locanda Orchidea € *Borgo degli Albizi, 11, 50122, Florence; Tel. (055) 2480346, fax 2480346.* There are only a few rooms in this budget hotel, housed very close to the Duomo, in the 12th-century palazzo in which Dante's wife was born. Furniture is old and quirky, only one of the rooms has a shower (the others share newly refurbished communal bathrooms), but the place has bags of character and the windows are huge, making the rooms light and airy. One room has a pretty terrace. Closed for most of August. 7 rooms. No credit cards.

Loggiato dei Serviti €€ *Piazza della SS Annunziata, 3, 50122 Florence; Tel. (055) 289592; fax 289595; <www.loggia-todeiservitihotel.it>.* The name recalls the 16th-century Servite monastery once housed in this palazzo with loggia, set on a beautifully-proportioned Renaissance piazza. Vaulted ceilings and imaginative design make each room unique. 29 rooms. Major credit cards.

Mario's €€ *Via Faenza, 89, 50123 Florence; Tel. (055) 216801, fax 212039, <www.webitaly.com/hotel.marios>.* Two blocks from the train station, this decades-old favorite is impeccably maintained, owned, and managed with warmth. Loyal clients keep coming back, and back again. 16 rooms. Major credit cards.

Monna Lisa €€€€ *Borgo Pinti, 27, 50121 Florence; Tel. (055) 247 9751; fax 247 9755.* In a landmark medieval palazzo, with original wooden ceilings, red-brick floors and lots of historical character. Rooms are generally small, the preferred (quieter) ones overlooking a central garden. Easy walk to both Duomo and Santa Croce. 30 rooms. Major credit cards.

Florence

Nuova Italia €–€€ *Via Faenza, 26, 50123 Florence; Tel. (055) 268430; fax 210941; e-mail <hotel.nuova.italia@dada.it>*. One of the more basic but comfortable family-friendly hotels in a lively area between the railway station and the street market near the Medici Chapels. Well run by a Florentine-American family that can never do enough for their guests. 20 rooms. Major credit cards.

Plaza Hotel Lucchesi €€€€ *Lungarno della Zecca Vecchia, 38, 50122, Florence; Tel. (055) 26236, fax 2480921; <www.plaza-lucchesi.it>*. Elegant and friendly hotel overlooking the river (river-view and terraced rooms must be specially requested), a few blocks east of the Uffizi. 97 rooms. Major credit cards.

Regency €€€€ *Piazza M. d'Azeglio, 3, 50121 Florence; Tel. (055) 245247; fax 2346735; <www.lordbyronhotel.com>*. A refined 19th-century style palazzo attractively distinguished with antiques and a much respected restaurant, situated on a leafy, quiet piazza in a residential corner of the city just east of the center. Quite a walk for those not accustomed. 34 rooms. Major credit cards.

Silla €€ *Via dei Renai, 5, 50125 Florence; Tel. (055) 2342888; fax 2341437.* Located in a seignorial 15th-century palazzo with much of its original detailing peeking through the recent renovations. On the Left Bank, one of its big draws is the large alfresco second-floor terrace for the perfect breakfast-with-a-view and afternoon aperitivo breaks. 35 rooms. Major credit cards.

Torre Guelfa €€ *Borgo Santissimi Apostoli, 8, 50123 Florence; Tel. (055) 2396338; fax 2398577, <www.firenzealbergo.it>*. On an ultra-central cobbled side street, in an early Renaissance palazzo built around a medieval tower with breathtaking 360-degree views. Most room have canopied beds; all have new bathrooms. 12 rooms. Major credit cards.

Recommended Restaurants

Central Florence is well supplied with cafés, bars, pizzerias, trattorias, and restaurants. The farther away from the tourist attractions you go, the less expensive they become. Many bars or cafés are beginning to offer light lunches as a trattoria alternative. Most restaurant bills will include a service charge (*servizio*) and a cover charge (*coperto*), and in this case it is usual to leave a small tip of a few coins for the waiter. If service is not included, it is because they are used to a tourist clientele: tip using your judgement as you would normally, 10–15 percent being the norm.

Below is a list of restaurants recommended by Berlitz; if you find other places worth including, we'd be pleased to hear from you. Reservations are recommended for the more expensive establishments. Almost all restaurants close during the summer's hottest weeks, usually from the end of July to 1 September for one to three weeks. Cafés below offer three (light) meals; unless specified all others offer lunch and dinner only. As a basic guide, we have used the following symbols to give an indication of the price of a three-course meal per person, including water and a bottle of house wine:

€€€€	over €65
€€€	€45–65
€€	€25–45
€	below €25

Acqua al Due € *Via di Vigna Vecchia, 40/r; Tel. (055) 284170.* Restaurant behind the Bargello known for its pasta: the signature dish is the pasta sampler plate with five varieties (with an occasional risotto thrown in). Second courses are available, but usually skipped to leave room for the dessert sampler. Relaxed and fun, a consistent mix of locals and tourists, students and families share communal tables. Daily, dinner. Major credit cards.

Florence

Alle Mossacce € *Via del Proconsolo, 55r; Tel. (055) 294361.* Traditional trattoria near the Duomo that has been here for more than 300 years with paper placemats and snap-to but kindly waiters who have been here longer than the furniture. The food is pure Tuscany — try a meal of *crostini* (toast spread with liver and anchovy paté), *ribollita* (vegetable soup thickened with bread), and *spezzatino alla fiorentina* (beef and tomato stew). An un-Tuscan specialty is their very good lasagna. Closed Saturday and Sunday. Major credit cards.

Angiolino €€ *Via Santo Spirito, 35/r; Tel. (055) 2398976.* Entertaining open kitchen displays excellent Tuscan dishes being prepared as they have been for the last 100 years. For generations a classic Florentine spot for Sunday dinner — timeless ambience guarantees an authentic experience. Locals order the house specialty *penne all'Angiolino* — short pasta dressed with a Chianti-accented tomato sauce. Closed Monday. Major credit cards.

Antellesi €€ *Via Faenza, 9/r; Tel. (055) 216990.* Authentic menu and well thought-out wine list. Try their aged *pecorino* with seasonal fruit and *crespelle alla fiorentina* (spinach and ricotta crepes with beschamel). The crown of Tuscan cuisine, *bistecca fiorentina*, is excellent here. Pair it with a great, reasonably priced Tuscan red. Daily. Major credit cards.

Borgo Antico € *Piazza Santo Spirito 6/r; Tel. (055) 210437. Reservations not accepted: first come, first served.* Jam-packed pizzeria known for great thin-crusted pizzas in a lively atmosphere. Young, often abrupt staff. There is a full menu as well, but grab a coveted outdoor piazza table and stick with a simple pizza, salad, and carafe of house wine. Daily. Major credit cards.

I Cafaggi €€ *Via Guelfa, 35/; Tel. (055) 294989.* Unassuming with great homemade family food; for decades on the short list of locals enjoying a night out. One place where you can also count on eating fish for a modest price. Lots of elbow rubbing with the locals, and good desserts. Closed Tuesdays. Major credit cards.

Caffè Gilli €€ *Via Roma, 1/r; Tel. (055) 213896; <www.gilli.it>.* Founded over 250 years ago, the Caffè Gilli is the plushest of all the cafés of the Piazza Repubblica. Redolent of a bygone era (particularly the old-fashioned interior), with its silver service and impeccable waiters. A traditional favorite place to rendez-vous, it is famous for its chocolates and especially its gianduja. **Caffè Paszkowski** (next door, closed Monday) is known for its summer evenings with live music. Closed on Tuesdays. Major credit cards.

Caffè Rivoire €€ *Piazza della Signoria 5; Tel. (055) 214412.* Arguably the most famous of all the history-steeped cafés for its ring-side seat in Florence's most picturesque piazza, with Michelangelo's *David* before you. Outside seating is perfect for iced tea, light lunch, and people watching. Thick, dark hot chocolate a local wintertime tradition. Activity flutters around the bar; proper service at the inside tables attract society's ladies of a certain age, along with foot-weary tourists. Closed Monday. Major credit cards.

Cantinetta Antinori €€€ *Palazzo Antinori, Piazza Antinori, 3; Tel. (055) 292234, fax 2359877; <www.antinori.it>.* This internationally known Tuscan wine producer invites you to dine in the alluring bar/restaurant of their august ancestral palazzo on the important Via Tornabuoni. Sit at the bar for a wine by-the-glass with a selection of regional cheeses, or request one of the 20 or so linen-covered tables for a simple, elegant meal. Closed Saturdays and Sundays. Major credit cards.

Cantinetta del Verrazzano € *Via dei Tavolini 18/20/r; Tel. (055) 268590.* Popular wine bar serving wines from the family vineyards in Chinati's Castello di Verrazzano. Great baked breads from the wood-burning ovens make this a great place to stop for a *merenda* (snack) or light meal, with a dozen or so Tuscan wines by-the-glass. Closed Sundays. Major credit cards.

Cantinone del Gallo Nero € *Via Santo Spirito, 6r; Tel. (055) 218898.* An inexpensive tavern with friendly communal tables, this *cantinone* (large wine cellar, which is what it was for centuries) offers a large selection of *antipasti*, various *crostini*, and good traditional poor-man dishes, such as a hearty peasant-like ribollita soup and *salsicce e fagioli* (a typical dish of sausage and beans). Closed Mondays. Major credit cards.

Casalinga € *Via Michelozzi, 9/; Tel. (055) 218624. Casalinga* means housewife so you know you are guaranteed a home-cooked meal here. One of the few places willing to serve you a *mezza porzione,* half portion, of any of their classic pasta dishes. Always busy, the staff is accomodating if not always smiling. Closed Sundays. Major credit cards.

I Che C'è C'è €€ *Via Magalotti, 11r; Tel. (055) 216589.* A rough translation of the name might be "we've got what we've got" — in other words, ask what today's special is. It's an enjoyable and friendly establishment that serves good Florentine fare such as ribollita, stracotto, and *coniglio ripieno* (rabbit stuffed with spinach and egg). Closed Monday. Major credit cards.

Il Latini €€ *Via Pachetti, 6/r; Tel. (055) 210916.* A lively, forever crowded Tuscan spot where comunal tables and plenty of people watching make the evening pass quickly. House cured *prosciutti* hang from the ceiling, and the platters of homemade pasta and typical Tuscan roasts parade out of the kitchen. The wines and oil come from the Latini family's Tuscan farm. Closed Monday. Major credit cards.

Il Cibreo Trattoria €€ *Via dei Macci, 118r; Tel. (055) 2341100.*
Simple, trattoria-style restaurant that adopts a modern approach to
classic Florentine dishes (i.e., no pasta) — *pappa al pomodoro* (a
thick garlic-flavored soup of bread and tomato), *piccione farcito con
mostarda di frutta* (pigeon stuffed with spiced fruit), *palombo gio-
vane alla livornese* (Livorno-style dove). Excellent desserts. The
adjacent restaurant is widely acclaimed: It shares the same kitchen,
but is far more expensive and formal and requires reservations, often far in advance. Closed Sunday and Monday. Major credit cards.

Coco Lezzone €€ *Via del Parioncino, 26r; Tel. (055) 287178;
fax 280349.* A small, popular, no-frills institution off the elite
shopping strip Via Tornabuoni, serving classic Florentine food
on small tables covered with red-and-white checked cloths. Try
the tasty pasta with porcini mushrooms. No credit cards and no
coffee. Closed Sunday. Major credit cards.

Dino €€–€€€ *Via Ghibellina, 51r; Tel. (055) 241452.* In the
Piazza Santa Croce neighborhood, a fine, traditional restaurant
whose menu is inspired in part by the peasant dishes of Tuscany,
in part by the noble banquets of the Medici — for the former try
trippa alla fiorentina (tripe in tomato sauce with parmesan), for
the latter *anguille del Papa Martino IV* (eels à la Pope Martin
IV!). Closed Sunday dinner, Monday. Major credit cards.

Enoteca Pinchiori €€€€ *Via Ghibellina, 87; Tel. (055)
242777.* One of the best and most famous restaurants in Italy,
with one of the world's greatest wine cellars. The gourmet menu
blends French and Tuscan influences. Think sparkling chande-
liers, silver cloches, and impeccable service. Dress formal.
Closed Sunday and Monday lunch. Major credit cards.

Le Fonticine €€€ *Via Nazionale, 79/r; Tel. (055) 282106.*
Large family-run trattoria at the far end of the outdoor San

Florence

Lorenzo market presents a marriage of Tuscan and Bolognese menus. Look for *tortellini al brodo* or *al ragu* (in broth or with meat sauce). There is also a pasta sampler for the hungry and curious. Closed Sundays, Mondays. Major credit cards.

Mamma Gina €€ *Borgo S. Jacopo, 37/; Tel. (055) 2396009; fax 213908*. Very respected Left Bank restaurant with fantastic wine list and proud staff that makes dinner in the brick-vaulted room memorable. Their bistecca fiorentina is perfectly grilled over flaming embers and their simple but perfect ribollita is one of the best in Florence. Closed Sundays. Major credit cards.

Osteria del Caffè Italiano € *Via Isola delle Stinche, 11/13/; Tel. (055) 289368*. A prodigious wine collection (also offered by the glass) with carefully matched local *salumi* (country-style salamis and cheeses) at the heavy oak bar. In an imposing early-Renaissance palazzo, this popular wine bar also proposes classic seasonal dishes including *mozzarella di buffalo* straight from Naples, and a great grilled menu, all served in a relaxed rustic atmosphere. It shares a kitchen with a full-fledged restaurant that offers a more varied menu and wine selection. Closed Mondays. Major credit cards.

Osteria del Cinghiale Bianco €€ *Borgo S. Jacopo, 43/r; Tel. (055) 215706*. Traditional dishes including hard-to-find namesake *cinghiale* (wild boar) are even tastier in the medieval, mood-setting ambience accented by a few romantic niche tables. If cinghiale is not your thing, there's a wide selection of simple classic Tuscan fare, even an American-style chef's salad, *insalata dello chef*. Great choice for Sunday or Monday when most other restaurants are closed. No credit cards. Closed Tuesdays and Wednesdays.

Pennello €€ *Via Dante Alighieri, 4r; Tel. (055) 294848; fax 294881*. Old-style trattoria around the corner from Dante's house (and therefore also referred to as Da Dante); said to be one of Florence's oldest restaurants. Known for its wide spread of fish and vegetable antipasti, and pasta, among other things. Closed Sunday evening, Monday. No credit cards.

Il Pizzaiolo € *Via dei Macci, 113/r; Tel (055) 241171.* Reservations are necessarry at this hopping pizzeria which offers just two seatings — at 8pm and at 9:30pm. A true Neopolitan *pizzaiolo* reigns over the wood-buring oven turning out thick chewy crusted individual pies. There is a regular trattoria menu offering traditional Tuscan fare, but pizza is a must — at least as a table-shared appetizer to start the evening off. No credit cards. Closed Sundays.

Sostanza €€ *Via della Porcellana, 25r; Tel. (055) 212691.* Established in 1869, this casual trattoria near Piazza Santa Maria Novella offers traditional country fare of minestrone, tripe, fried chicken, and stracotto, but most come for the acclaimed bistecca fiorentina (after all, this place originated as a butcher shop). Vegetarians revel in the *frittata di carciofi* (artichoke omelette) in season. No credit cards. Closed Saturday, Sunday.

13 Gobbi €€ *Via Porcellana 9/r; Tel (055) 284015.* On the same block as Sostanza, the quirkily named "13 Hunchbacks" offers a dim, relaxed atmosphere with a warm and helpful staff. Innovative, hearty dishes such as *tagliata di bistecca all'aceto balsamico* (sliced steak dressed with balsamic vinegar) are paired with choice wines not always on the menu. Closed Monday lunch. Major credit cards.

Zà-Zà €€ *Piazza Mercato Centrale, 26/; Tel. (055) 215411.* Traditional Tuscan fare served at communal wooden tables frequented by tourists and market-vendors and -goers alike. Try the *crostini misti*, ribollita, or the famous bistecca.

INDEX